Study Guide
for

Biopsychology
Third Edition

Michael J. Mana
Chatham College

John P.J. Pinel
University of British Columbia

Allyn and Bacon
Boston • London • Toronto • Sydney • Tokyo • Singapore

TABLE OF CONTENTS

INTRODUCTION

This study guide is intended to increase your enjoyment of BIOPSYCHOLOGY, and to improve your grades by helping you to focus on and remember the key points of the text. Its design is based on the following four principles of good study:

Active Studying: Studying is far more effective when it is active. Many students prepare for examinations by simply reading the assigned material over and over, but such attempts to passively absorb material are not very productive. Studies have repeatedly shown that acquisition, comprehension, and retention are all better when the student interacts actively with the material by writing out answers to key questions or by thinking the answers through.

Bidirectional Studying: In order to be fully prepared, a student must study bidirectionally. Many students actively prepare for examinations by repeatedly reviewing a set of study questions. Because most questions about specific points can be posed in two opposite ways, students who study in this manner may be unable to answer questions about the points that they have studied if they are posed in the opposite way. For example, a student who can successfully answer the question, "Who is John Pinel?" may not be able to answer the question, "Who is the author of this study guide?". The Jeopardy section of each chapter in this study guide specifically focuses on bidirectional study habits.

Multiple-level Studying: Effective study focuses on different levels of detail. Some students study by reviewing details while others study by thinking about general concepts and issues. However, in neither of these cases does the student gain a complete grasp of the material, and in neither case is the student prepared to write an examination that includes a variety of different kinds of test items. In order to be fully prepared, it is necessary to study both detail and general concepts and issues.

Formal Pretesting: The best way for a student to assess the progress of her or his studying is to write a practice examination. The results of a practice examination written under self-imposed examination conditions a day or two before a scheduled examination will indicate the areas that require special last-minute review. Each chapter in this study guide contains a full-lenght practice examination, much like the ones that we have used in our own classes.

There Are Three Sections in Each Chapter of This Study Guide

There are 17 chapters in this study guide, each of which is associated with one of the 17 chapters of BIOPSYCHOLOGY. Each chapter of this study guide includes the following three sections.

Section I: Jeopardy Study Items

For the lack of a better name, I have named the first items in each chapter of the study guide "jeopardy study items" after Jeopardy, the popular television quiz show. This quiz show differs from other quiz shows in that the contestants are given the answers and are asked to come up with the correct questions. The jeopardy items in each chapter are arranged in two columns, with the questions in the left column and the answers in the right. Sometimes there is nothing in the space to the right of a question, and your task is to fill the space with the correct answer; sometimes there is nothing in the space to the left of an answer, and your task is to fill the space with the correct question. In order to insure that your answers and questions are correct, you should use your text to complete these items. What you will have when you have completed this section is a series of questions and answers that summarize the key points in each chapter. Moreover, they will be conveniently arranged on the page so that you can readily practice bidirectional studying: Cover the right column and practice anticipating the correct answers to each question, and then cover the left column and practice anticipating the correct questions to each answer.

Section II: Essay Study Questions

The purpose of the essay study questions is to make sure that you do not fail to see the forest for the trees; their purpose is to focus your attention on general principles, concepts, and issues. The essay study questions cover much of the same material as do the jeopardy study items, but they do so at a more general level of analysis.

Section III: Practice Examination

In the third and last section of each chapter is a practice examination, which is intended to help you assess the progress of your studying. Each practice examination is composed of several kinds of questions: multiple-choice questions, fill-in-the-blanks questions, modified true-false questions, short-answer questions, and diagram questions. After writing a practice examination, mark it -- the answers are at the end of each study guide chapter -- and use your performance on the practice examination to plan the final stages of your studying.

How to Use This Study Guide To Prepare for an Examination

The recommended method for using this study guide involves the following eight steps:

1. Read the assigned chapter from BIOPSYCHOLOGY. Underline particularly important or difficult parts as you read.

2. Using BIOPSYCHOLOGY, complete the jeopardy study items in the appropriate chapter of the study guide. These items are arranged in the order in which they appear in the text to make it easy for you to complete them.

3. Study the jeopardy study items by covering up the left half of each page and thinking through the correct answer to each covered question. Then, cover the right half of each page and think through the correct question for every covered answer. Repeat until your performance is error free. Each time that you fail to correctly anticipate a question or answer, put an asterisk next to it so that you can focus on these items during the final phases of your studying.

4. Using BIOPSYCHOLOGY, write the outline of your best answer to each essay study question. Memorize each outline. Put an asterisk next to any essay question that gives you a problem.

5. Read through the assigned chapter again, focusing on what you have previously underlined. Before you turn a page, try to anticipate and think through all of the underlined points on the next page. Place an asterisk next to any point that you have trouble anticipating.

6. Study the list of key words at the end of the chapter in BIOPSYCHOLOGY. Practice bidirectional studying until you can go from term to definition and from definition to term without making an error. Each time that you miss a term or definition, put an asterisk next to it.

7. Write the appropriate practice examination in this study guide at least 24 hours before you are scheduled to write your formal examination. Grade your practice examination by referring to the correct answers that follow it. Place an asterisk next to each item that you get wrong.

8. On the basis of your performance on the practice examination, plan the final phases of your studying. At some point during the last day of preparation, make sure that you can respond correctly to each point with an asterisk next to it.

Dear Student:

I do hope that this study guide will make BIOPSYCHOLOGY a more worthwhile and enjoyable experience for you, but I am not going to wish you good luck in your quest for knowledge and high grades. If you put this study guide to good use, you will not need good luck.

If you have any comments, suggestions, or questions about this study guide or about BIOPSYCHOLOGY, please write to me at the Department of Psychology, 2136 West Mall, University of British Columbia, Vancouver, B.C., Canada V6T 1Z4.

Cordially,

John Pinel

Greetings...

I was a graduate student in John Pinel's lab when he announced his intention to write a textbook. Over the next couple of years I watched as the first edition of BIOPSYCHOLGY came together, helping with the literature searches and the proof-reading that were involved with each chapter. I graduated in time to use the first edition of BIOPSYCHOLOGY in the first class that I taught; since then, I have kept in contact with John and watched with interest as he completed the second edition of BIOPSYCHOLOGY, which also became the cornerstone for many of the classes that I taught.

Now BIOPSYCHOLOGY is in its third edition, and I am happy to once again be a part of the process. I hope that this revision of the study guide helps you to better understand the material presented in BIOPSYCHOLOGY. If you have any questions or comments pleace contact me at the Department of Biology, Chatham College, Woodland Drive, Pittsburgh, PA 15232. I can also be contacted electronically at: MANA@CHATHAM.EDU.

All the Best,

Mike Mana

Michael J. Mana, Ph.D.

Chapter 1

BIOPSYCHOLOGY AS A NEUROSCIENCE

I.   Jeopardy Study Items

With reference to Chapter 1 of BIOPSYCHOLOGY, write the correct answer to each of the following questions and the correct question for each of the following answers.

1. What is neuroscience?

2. Who was Jimmie G.?

3.   This is a branch of neuroscience concerned with how the
                                                 nervous system controls behavior.

4. Who was D.O. Hebb?

5. What is biopsychology?

6. What unique contribution does biopsychology make to neuroscience?

7. Biopsychology is greatly influenced by six other subdisciplines of neuroscience. Define each of these subdisciplines; when you are provided with a definition, provide the name of the subdiscipline. (p. 5)

    a. neuroanatomy

    b.   This is the study of the responses of the nervous system, particularly those involved in transmission of electrical signals through and between neurons.

    c. neurochemistry

    d.   This is the study of nervous system disorders.

    e. neuropharmacology

    f.   This is the study of the interactions of the nervous system with the endocrine glands and the hormones they release.

7. Why does neuroscientific research often focus on nonhuman animals?

8. What is the difference between a within-subjects design and a between-subjects design?

9. What are the following three kinds of experimental variables?

    a.   independent variable

    b.   This is the variable measured by the experimenter.

    c.   confounded variable

10.   This refers to the observation that sexually fatigued animals will often recommence copulation if a new sex partner is provided.

11. Define or name the following three types of research?

    a.   experiment

    b.   This is a study in which subjects are not assigned to conditions, but are studied in real-world conditions

    c.   This is the study of a single subject.

12.   This type of study is limited by its generalizability.

13. What is the difference between pure research and applied research?

14. Why do many scientists believe that pure research will ultimately provide more practical benefit than applied research?

15. Define or name the following five divisions of biopsychology?

    a. physiological psychology

    b.   This is the study of effects of drugs on behavior and how they
                                          are mediated by the nervous system.

    c. neuropsychology

    d.   This is the study of the relationship between physiological
                                          processes and psychological processes in humans.

    e. comparative psychology

16.   This is the study of an animal's behavior in its natural
                                          environment.

17. What is the concept of converging operations?

18.   This is the method that scientists use to study the
                                          unobservable.

19. Why should you be aware of previous errors in
    biopsychological research?

20. What is the most reasonable interpretation of Delgado's
    charging-bull demonstration?

21. What is Morgan's Canon?

22. What is a prefrontal lobotomy?

23. Who were Moniz and Lima?

24. Who was Becky, and what is her claim to fame in the field of biopsychology?

25. What were some of the undesirable side effects of the prefrontal lobotomy procedure?

Once you have completed the jeopardy study items, study them. Practice bidirectional studying; make sure that you know the correct answer to every question and the correct question for every answer.

II.   Essay Study Questions

Using Chapter 1 of BIOPSYCHOLOGY, write an outline to answer to each of the following essay study questions.

1. In the *Organization of Behavior,* Hebb combined research on animals and humans with clinical and day-to-day observations to support his theory that psychological phenomena could be produced by the activity of the brain. How is this eclectic approach reflected in current biopsychological inquiry?

2. How do biopsychologists use observational methods to study unobservable phenomena? Give an example.

3. What are the advantages and disadvantages of humans vs. nonhuman animals as subjects in neuroscientific research?

4. Compare and contrast experiments, quasiexperimental studies, and case studies.

5. Compare and contrast the five divisions of biopsychology.

6. Describe the case of caudate stimulation and the charging bull. What does this case teach us about good and bad science?

7. Describe the development of prefrontal lobotomy as a treatment for psychological dysfunction. What lessons does this episode teach us about good and bad science?

When you have answered the essay study questions, memorize your outlines to prepare for your upcoming examination.

III.   Practice Examination

After completing most of your studying of Chapter 1, but at least 24 hours before your formal examination, write the following practice examination.

A. Multiple-Choice Section. Circle the correct answer for each question; *REMEMBER that some questions may have more than one correct answer.*

1. Biopsychology can be considered to be a division of:

    a. physiological psychology.
    b. neuroscience.
    c. neuroanatomy.
    d. neurophysiology.

2. According to the text, who played the major role in the emergence of biopsychology as a discipline?

    a. Lashley
    b. Moniz
    c. Hebb
    d. Sperry

3. Korsakoff's syndrome is:

    a. characterized by severe memory loss.
    b. caused by damage to the frontal lobes of the brain.
    c. caused by alcohol-induced toxicity of neural tissue.
    d. caused by a thiamin (vitamin B1) deficiency.

4. The diversity of biopsychological research is reflected in the fact that:

    a. it can involve animal or human subjects.
    b. it can involve experiments or nonexperimental studies.
    c. it generally focuses on the integrative activity of whole organisms.
    d. it can focus on either pure or applied research.

5. A comparison between the performance of alcoholics and that of age-matched nonalcoholics on a test of memory would qualify as:

    a. a quasiexperimental study.
    b. an experiment.
    c. a case study.
    d. a within-subject study.

6. Research aimed at developing better psychotherapeutic drugs is:

    a. applied research.
    b. psychopharmacological research.
    c. pure research.
    d. rarely done with nonhuman subjects.

7. The effects of electrical brain stimulation on the behavior of rats would most likely be studied by a:

    a. comparative psychologist.
    b. psychopharmacologist.
    c. psychophysiologist.
    d. physiological psychologist

8. The study of the integrated behavior of whole, functioning, adapted organisms describes the subdiscipline of:

    a. psychobiology
    b. comparative psychology
    c. neuropsychology
    d. psychopharmacology

9. Merton was both the experimenter and the subject in a classic experiment on eye movement. Merton's eye muscles were curarized, and then when he tried to look to the right:

    a. his eyes actually moved to the left.
    b. his eyes moved to the right, but even farther than intended.
    c. everything in his visual field seemed to move to the right.
    d. everything in his visual field seemed to move to the left.

10. Delgado's demonstration that caudate stimulation prevented the charge of a raging bull supports the idea that:

    a. Delgado had located the taming center of the bull's brain.
    b. Delgado had located a neural pathway controlling movement.
    c. Delgado had confused the bull.
    d. caudate stimulation could be used to calm human psychopaths.

B. Modified True-False and Fill-in-the Blank Section. If the statement is true, write TRUE in the blank provided. If the statement is false, write FALSE as well as the word or words that will make the statement true if they replaced the highlighted word or words in the original statement. If the statement is incomplete, write the word or words that will complete it.

1. True or False: **Mice** are the most common nonhuman subjects in biopsychology experiments.

        A: _____

2. By definition, a confounded variable is an unintended difference between the conditions of an experiment that can affect the **independent** variable.

        A: _____

3. In their well-controlled study, Lester and Gorzalka (1988) demonstrated that the Coolidge effect is not restricted to _____.

4. True or False: The amnesiac effect of alcohol abuse results, to a large degree, from **alcohol-induced neurotoxicity.**

        A: _____

5. Neuropsychology is largely focused on the study of the effects of damage to _____ on human behavior.

6. The measure of brain activity most often recorded by psychophysiologists is the scalp _____.

7. Progress is most rapid when different research approaches are brought to bear on the same problem. This approach is called _____.

8. Scientists find out about unobservable phenomena by drawing scientific _____ from events that they can observe.

9. The discipline of neuroscience that specializes in the study of nervous system disorders is called
_____.

10. The disaster of _____ as a therapeutic form of psychosurgery emphasizes the need to carefully evaluate the consequences of such procedures on the first patients to receive such an operation.

C. Short Answer Section. In no more than 4 sentences, answer each of the following questions.

1. Chapter 1 of BIOPSYCHOLOGY concludes with two examples of bad science: one about prefrontal lobotomy and the other about raging bulls. For each "rule of good research" provided below, describe how each example described in Chapter 1 violates the qualities of good scientific protocol.

   a. In interpreting behavior, Morgan's Canon should always be heeded.

   b. Researchers should be especially cautious when involved in the objective evaluation of their own efforts.

   c. It is important to test any putative therapeutic procedure on a variety of species before using it as a treatment for human disorders.

2. The use of nonhuman subjects instead of human subjects has several advantages in biopsychological research; describe each of the advantages.

Mark your answers to the practice examination; the correct answers follow. On the basis of your performance, plan the final stages of your studying.

Answers to Practice Examination

Multiple Choice Section

1. b	6. a, b
2. c	7. d
3. a, d	8. b
4. a, b, d	9. c
5. a	10. b

B. Modified True/False and Fill-in-the-Blank Section

1. a
2. thiamin
3. neurotoxin
4. d
5. e
6. c
7. electroencephalogram (or EEG)
8. converging operations
9. inferences
10. c

C. Short Answer Section

1. Mention the similarities between the brains of human and nonhuman species; the benefits of a comparative approach to the study of behavior; the ethical considerations that restrict many kinds of experimentation on human beings.

2. a) Mention Morgan's Canon, and how in each case the simplest explanation for the data was ignored for something that the experimenters wanted to believe to be true.

    b) Mention the lack of objectivity that was implicit in the conclusions that each group of researchers reached about their work.

    c) Mention the dangers in rushing a new procedure into use as a therapeutic tool before it is thoroughly tested.

Chapter 2

EVOLUTION, GENETICS, AND DEVELOPMENT: ASKING THE RIGHT QUESTIONS ABOUT THE BIOLOGY OF BEHAVIOR

I.   Jeopardy Study Items

With reference to Chapter 2 of BIOPSYCHOLOGY, write the correct answer to each of the following questions and the correct question for each of the following answers

1. What is a Zeitgeist?

2.   A: This idea grew out of a seventeenth-century conflict between science and the Roman church.

3. What was Cartesian dualism, and what effect did it have?

4.   A: This debate is often referred to as the nature-nurture issue.

5.   A: He was the father of *behaviorism.*

6. Two kinds of evidence contradict physiological-or-psychological thinking. What are they?

7. What is *ethology?*

8. What is asomatognosia?

9. What evidence suggests that chimpanzees are self-aware?

10. How has nature-or-nurture thinking evolved?

11. All behavior is the product of interactions among three factors. What are they?

12. What three kinds of evidence did Darwin offer to support his theory of evolution?

13. What is natural selection?

14. What did Darwin mean by fitness?

15. What is the relationship between the terms *species* and *conspecific?*

16. What role does social dominance play in evolution?

17. How do courtship displays promote the evolution of new species?

18. What is the definition of a *chordate?*

19. Organize the following classes of vertebrates according to the time of the phylogenetic development: fishes; amphibians; reptiles; mammals.

20. How and why did land-dwelling vertebrates evolve from fishes?

21.   A: It is the duck-billed platypus.

22. What is a mammal?

23.   A: This order includes prosimians, new-world monkeys, old-world monkeys, apes, and hominids.

24. What developmental alteration allows mammals the opportunity for more complex programs of development to unfold?

25.   A: This was *Homo erectus*.

26. How old is the species *Homo sapiens?*

27. What evidence suggests that brain size is not a good measure of intellectual capacity?

28. Why is it better to consider the evolution of the brain stem and cerebrum independently?

29. What are 3 key points about the evolution of the human brain?

30.   A: This is the functional approach to the study of brain-behavior relationships.

31.   A: This is the comparative approach to the study of brain-behavior relationships.

32. What the two key decisions that led to Mendel's success in his research on inheritance in pea plants?

33.   A: Because it challenged the premise that offspring inherit the traits of their parents.

34. What is a gene?

35. What is the difference between genotype and phenotype?

36.   A: homozygous and heterozygous?

37.   A: You have 23 pairs of them.

38. What is the function of mitosis?

39. What is the function of meiosis?

40. Why is the phenomenon of crossing over important?

41.   A: These chromosomes do not come in matched pairs

42. How are gene maps constructed from studies of linkage?

43.   A: This is the reason why the number of thymine bases equals the number of adenine bases, and the number of guanine bases equals the number of cytosine bases.

44. Why do recessive sex-linked trains occur more often in males?

45. How does DNA self-duplicate?

46.   A: These are structural genes and operator genes.

47. What is a protein?

48. What is one way that the environment can interact with genes to alter the course of development?

49. Why was the "cross fostering" control procedure important to Tryon's work?

50. What important caveat should you keep in mind when assessing studies of selective breeding?

51. What is the mechanism of PKU?

52.   A: Sensitive period.

53. How is the size of a bird's neural song structures related
    to its ability to sing?

54. Why is the seasonal change in the neural structures that
    underlie birdsong in the canary so remarkable?

55.   A: monozygotic and dizygotic twins

56. What have been the major findings of the Minnesota
    study of twins reared apart?

57.   A: heritability estimates

58. How do genetic differences promote psychological
    differences?

Once you have completed the jeopardy study items, study them. Practice bidirectional studying; make sure
that you know the correct answer to every question and the correct question for every answer.

II. Essay Study Questions

Using Chapter 2 of BIOPSYCHOLOGY, write an outline to answer to each of the following essay study questions.

1. People tend to think about the biology of behavior in terms of two dichotomies. What are they, and what is wrong with these ways of thinking?

2. Describe the three-factor model that illustrates the way that many contemporary biopsychologists think about behavior?

3. Discuss efforts to study the evolution of the human brain.

4. Describe Mendel's classic experiment and the theory that he developed to explain it.

5. Discuss the relation among crossing over, linkage, and gene maps.

6. Describe how Tryon's research undermined the idea that behavior is largely the result of experience.

7. What is a heritability estimate? What does it mean, and what does it not mean? Discuss with respect to the Minnesota Study of Twins Reared Apart.

8. Behavioral capacities are the product of the interaction between genetics and experience. Illustrate this idea with reference to maze-bright and maze-dull rats, phenylketonuria, and bird song.

9. What is the key difference between the development of individuals and the development of differences between individuals?

When you have answered the essay study questions, memorize your outlines to prepare for your upcoming examination

III.   Practice Examination

> *After completing most of your studying of Chapter 2, but at least 24 hours before your formal examination, write the following practice examination.*

A. Multiple-Choice Section. Circle the correct answer for each question; *REMEMBER that some questions may have more than one correct answer.*

1. Gallup studied the self-awareness of chimpanzees by studying their reactions to:

   a. their images in a mirror.
   b. odorless red dots that had been painted on their eyebrow ridges while they were anesthetized.
   c. photographs of conspecifics.
   d. their interactions with one another.

2. According to Darwin, the mechanism of evolution is:

   a. linkage.
   b. natural selection.
   c. crossing over.
   d. aggressive display.

3. Which encourages the evolution of new species?

   a. courtship display
   b. social dominance
   c. aggressive behavior
   d. defensive behavior

4. Research has shown that canaries are:

   a. *age-limited* learners of their song repertoires.
   b. *open-ended* learners of their song repertoires.
   c. are particularly effective in learning songs that they hear when they are between 10 and 50 days of age.
   d. return to a state of plastic song production at the end of each summer.

5. The canary song circuit is remarkable because:

   a. the left descending motor circuit is more important than the right descending motor circuit.
   b. the high vocal center is larger in females than males.
   c. the neural substrates underlying song production double in size each spring.
   d. the increase in the size of the neural substrates underlying song production reflects an increase in the size of existing neurons in these areas.

6. Cartesian dualism marked a critical point in the study of brain and behavior because:

   a. it gave one part of the universe to science and the other part to the Church.
   b. it separated the physical function of the body from the function of the mind.
   c. it suggested that the mind was a suitable subject for scientific investigation.
   d. it resolved the conflict between scientific knowledge and Church dogma that existed during the Renaissance.

7. In his monumental work *The Origin of Species,* Charles Darwin:

   a. was the first to propose that new species evolve from preexisting species.
   b. initiated the modern science of biology.
   c. was the first to suggest how evolution occurs.
   d. explained the role of Mendelian genetics in evolution.

8. As far as we can tell, the first hominids to produce works of art were:

   a. Cro-Magnons.
   b. Neanderthals.
   c. Homo sapiens.
   d. the Grateful Dead.

9. In selective breeding experiments, the possibility that behavioral characteristics are being transmitted from parent to offspring through learning is controlled for by:

   a. restricting the experiment to subjects of just one sex.
   b. using a cross-fostering procedure.
   c. restricting such research to the study of twins.
   d. raising the subjects in an enriched environment.

10. Sex-linked traits are:

    a. the product of chromosomes that do not come in matched pairs.
    b. almost always controlled by the Y chromosome.
    c. often more common in males if they are due to a recessive gene.
    d. controlled by genes on the sex chromosomes.

11. The control of gene expression is:

    a. under the control of operator genes.
    b. regulated by DNA-binding proteins.
    c. not sensitive to the environment that an organism exists in.
    d. important to the way a cell develops and then functions once it has reached maturity.

12. According to the Minnesota Twins test, identical twins were:

    a. similar in intelligence and personality only if they were raised together.
    b. similar in both intelligence and personality regardless of whether or not they were raised together.
    c. so similar that the results proved that intelligence and personality are inherited traits.
    d. similar in every trait that the researchers chose to study.

B. Modified True-False and Fill-in-the Blank Section. If the statement is true, write TRUE in the blank provided. If the statement is false, write FALSE as well as the word or words that will make the statement true if they replaced the highlighted word or words in the original statement. If the statement is incomplete, write the word or words that will complete it.

1. The first mammals were egg-laying reptiles with _____ glands.

2. Mendel's experiments succeeded because he studied _____ traits and _____ lines.

3. True or False: **Twin studies** provide an estimate of the proportion of variability occurring in a particular trait in a particular study that resulted from the genetic variation in that study.

    A: _____

The base sequence one strand of a DNA molecule is provided in the following list. What is the complementary base sequence on the other strand?

4.   cytosine - _____
5.   guanine - _____
6.   adenine - _____
7.   thymine - _____
8.   guanine - _____

9. The hormone _____ has been implicated in the annual cycle of death and growth of song-circuit neurons.

10. True or False: Gametes are produced by **mitosis;** all other body cells are produced by the process of **meiosis.**

    A: _____

11. _____ are the closest living relatives of human beings; about _____ of the genetic material is identical in these two species.

12. Each _____ of a _____ gene instructs the ribosome to add a particular _____ to the _____ that it is constructing.

13. Diamond's finding that PKU children on special diets still performed poorly on a variety of cognitive tests suggests that these children still suffer from damage to the _____ of the brain.

14. PKU is an inherited disorder caused by the absence of the enzyme _____.

15. True or False: The best way to study brain evolution is to compare the **weight and size** of different brain regions.

    A: _____

16. European ethology focused on the study of _____ behaviors.

17. To support his theory of evolution, Darwin pointed out the evolution of _____ through progressively more recent geological layers, the striking _____ similarities of different living species, and the major changes that can be produced in a species by _____.

18. The recessive variant of a dichotomous trait will appear in _____ of the second-generation offspring.

19. Chromosomes exist in the _____ of each cell.

20. The most common errors in the duplication of chromosomes are referred to as _____.

21. Copper and Zubek (1958) demonstrated that _____ can overcome the negative effects of disadvantaged genes.

22. True or False: Drugs that elevate levels of **phenylalanine** in the prefrontal cortex may be useful in the treatment of PKU.

    A: _____

23. Young males of many species are genetically prepared to acquire the songs of their own species during the _____ of song acquisition.

24. Two major neural pathways are involved in birdsong in the canary: the _____ mediates the production of song while the _____ mediates the acquisition of song.

25. True or False: Selective breeding studies in animals and twin studies in humans have revealed **several key psychological differences** that do not have a significant genetic component.

    A: _____

C. Short Answer Section. In no more than 4 sentences, answer each of the following questions.

1. Discuss the statement "Tryon's selectively bred rats were especially good at maze-running because of their superior intelligence".

2. The study of overall brain size is not a good way to approach the evolution of intellect. Why?

3. Describe the functional approach and the comparative approach to the study of brain-behavior relationships.

4. Describe the two key phases of birdsong acquisition and the differences between age-limited learners and open-ended learners.

5. The Minnesota Twins study was misinterpreted in four important ways. Discuss each of these misinterpretations.

Mark your answers to the practice examination; the correct answers follow. On the basis of your performance, plan the final stages of your studying...

Answers to Practice Examination

A. Multiple Choice Section

1. a, b	7. b, c
2. b	8. c
3. a	9. b
4. b, d	10. a, c, d
5. a, c	11. a, b, d
6. a, b, c	12. b

B. Modified True/False and Fill-in-the-Blank Section

1. mammary
2. dichotomous; true-breeding
3. F: heritability estimates
4. guanine
5. cytosine
6. thymine
7. adenine
8. cytosine
9. testosterone
10. F: meiosis; mitosis
11. Chimpanzees; 99%
12. codon; structural; amino acid; protein
13. prefrontal cortex
14. phenyalanine hydroxylase
15. F: evolution
16. instinctive
17. fossil layers; structural; selective breeding
18. about a quarter
19. nucleus
20. mutations
21. enriched environments
22. F: dopamine
23. sensory phase
24. descending motor pathway; ascending forebrain pathway
25. F: no psychological differences

C. Short Answer Section

1. Mention the inaccuracy of this statement in light of Searle's research and his findings; the fact that selective breeding often alters many different traits.

2. Mention the fact that humans do not have the largest brains, in absolute or relative (brain weight/body weight index) terms; the lack of correlation between intelligence and brain size; the advantages of considering the evolution of different parts of the brain.

3. Mention the emphasis of the functional approach on evolutionary pressures; the emphasis of the comparative approach on different species; the ideas that human beings are the products of evolution and our phylogenetic ancestors.

4. Mention sensory and sensorimotor phases of song acquisition; the importance of early experience; contrast the closed repertoire of age-limited songbirds to the ever-changing repertoire of open-ended songbirds.

5. Mention the focus on nature-nurture; the focus on similarities instead of differences; the lack of novelty in the findings; and the misinterpretation of what a heritability estimate means.

Chapter 3

THE ANATOMY OF THE NERVOUS SYSTEM

I.   Jeopardy Study Items

With reference to Chapter 3 of BIOPSYCHOLOGY, write the correct answer to each of the following questions and the correct question for each of the following answers

1. What defines the border between the central nervous system and the peripheral nervous system?

2.   A: The somatic nervous system and the autonomic nervous system.

3. What is the difference between efferent and afferent nerves?

4. What is the main difference between the functions of the sympathetic and the parasympathetic nervous systems?

5.   A: The 12 cranial nerves.

6. Which cranial nerves are involved with vision?

7. What is meant by the statement "The nervous system is a system of twos."?

8.   A: These are called dura mater, arachnoid membrane, and pia mater.

9. Where is CSF created, and where does it flow?

10. People who have lost some of their CSF suffer from what kind of symptoms?

11. What is hydrocephalus?

12. What is the blood-brain barrier?

13.   A: Neurons and support cells.

14. What are neurons?

15. What are the major external features of a typical neuron?

16.   A: This type of neuron has little or no axonal process.

17. What are nuclei, ganglia, tracts, and nerves?

18.   A: Glial cells and satellite cells.

19. Why is there normally little axonal regeneration in the mammalian CNS?

20. Describe the Golgi technique and tell why it was such a revolutionary technique for early neuroanatomists?

21.   A: This type of stain only marks structures in neuron cell bodies.

22. What is the difference between anterograde and retrograde tract tracing?

23. In the nervous system, what is another name for the following terms: anterior; posterior; frontal.

24.   A: midsagittal section

25. What are the names of the four arms of gray matter visible in a cross section of the spinal cord?

26.   A: dorsal root ganglia

27. From anterior to posterior, name the five major divisions
    of the human brain.

28. What is the other name for midbrain?

29. Which division of the human brain undergoes the greatest
    amount of growth during development?

30.   A: sleep, attention, movement, maintenance of muscle tone,
                                           cardiac and respiratory reflexes

31.   A: cerebellum and pons.

32. What are the four structures of the mammalian tectum?
    What are their functions?

33. Where is the periaqueductal gray? What role does it
    have in the effects of opiate drugs?

34.   A: massa intermedia

35.   A: lateral geniculate, medial geniculate, and ventral posterior
                                           nuclei.

36.   A: It was once known as the snot gland.

37. Name the four lobes of the cerebral hemispheres?

38. What does *lissencephalic* mean?

39. What is the corpus callosum?

40.   A: It has six layers of cells.

41. Describe three important characteristics of neocortex anatomy.

42. Name the structures that make up the limbic system.

43.   A: globus pallidus, putamen, caudate, and amygdala

44. What is the relationship between the amygdala, the limbic system, and the basal ganglia?

45. What is the striatum, and how is it related to Parkinson's disease?

Once you have completed the jeopardy study items, study them. Practice bidirectional studying; make sure that you know the correct answer to every question and the correct question for every answer.

II.   Essay Study Questions

Using Chapter 3 of BIOPSYCHOLOGY, write an outline of the answer to each of the following essay study questions.

1. Draw and label all major parts of a typical neuron.

2. Compare and contrast the function of oligodendroglia in the CNS and Schwann cells in the PNS?

3. Describe how the Golgi stain, Nissl stains, myelin stains, and electron microscopy are used in the study of the anatomy of the nervous system.

4. Compare techniques that are used for anterograde and retrograde tracing in the nervous system.

5. Name the structures that comprise the basal ganglia, and describe the function of this system.

6. Describe the anatomy and function of the afferent and efferent branches of the peripheral nervous system.

7. Describe the embryological development of the five major divisions of the brain.

8. What are the five major divisions of the human brain, and what are their major structures?

9. What is the reticular activating center?

When you have answered the essay study questions, memorize your outlines to prepare for your upcoming examination.

III. Practice Examination

> *After completing most of your studying of Chapter 3, but at least 24 hours before your formal examination, write the following practice examination.*

A. Multiple-Choice Section. Circle the correct answer for each question; *REMEMBER that some questions may have more than one correct answer.*

1. The first two cranial nerves in the mammalian brain are the:

    a. vagus and trigeminal nerves.
    b. olfactory and optic nerves.
    c. vagus and olfactory nerves.
    d. optic and vagus nerves.

2. Between the arachnoid membrane and the pia mater membrane, there:

    a. are large blood vessels.
    b. is the subarachnoid space.
    c. is CSF.
    d. are cerebral ventricles

3. The function of CSF is:

    a. to filter the blood before it enters the brain.
    b. to support and cushion the brain.
    c. ensure that the cortex does not collapse into the ventricles.
    d. moisten the brain.

4. The Nissl stains stain:

    a. only a few neurons in each section.
    b. neurons completely black.
    c. neurons in their entirety, but not glia.
    d. all of the above

5. Which of the following terms can refer to two totally different structures in the nervous system?

    a. tract
    b. nucleus
    c. nerve
    d. ganglion

6. A section cut in which of the following planes could include both eyes?

    a. horizontal
    b. coronal
    c. frontal
    d. all of the above

7. The periaqueductal gray, the red nucleus, and the substantia nigra are all part of the:

    a. tegmentum.
    b. mesencephalon.
    c. diencephalon.
    d. both a and b

8. The massa intermedia and the lateral geniculate nuclei are part of the:

    a. myelencephalon.
    b. metencephalon.
    c. telencephalon.
    d. diencephalon.

9. The proteins that are embedded in the lipid bilayer that comprises the neural membrane may be:

    a. neurotransmitters
    b. channel proteins
    c. signal proteins
    d. myelin

10. The hippocampus is:

    a. neocortex
    b. has only three cell layers
    c. located in the temporal lobe
    d. pyramidal shaped.

B. Modified True-False and Fill-in-the Blank Section. If the statement is true, write TRUE in the blank provided. If the statement is false, write FALSE as well as the word or words that will make the statement true if they replaced the highlighted word or words in the original statement. If the statement is incomplete, write the word or words that will complete it.

According to neuroanatomical arithmetic:

1. PNS - ANS = _____ nervous system

2. CNS - brain = _____

3. sympathetic + parasympathetic = _____

4. Are sensory nerves efferent or afferent? _____

5. The third and fourth ventricles are connected by the _____.

6. The nervous system contains three different categories of neurons: sensory neurons, motor neurons, and

    _____.

7. The three protective membranes that enclose the brain and spinal cord are called the _____,
   the _____, and the _____.

8. Axonal regeneration in the PNS is possible because _____ guide the regenerating
   axons.

9. The corpus callosum and all the other commissures would be transected by a _____ cut
   through the brain.

10. The optic chiasm is the structure through which axons of some visual-system neurons _____.

11. True or False: The two major structures of the metencephalon are the **thalamus and hypothalamus.**

        A: _____

12. The basal ganglia motor system includes the amygdala, the striatum, and the _____.

13. True or False: The **colliculi** are a pair of hypothalamic nuclei visible as bumps on the ventral or inferior surface
    of the human brain.

        A: _____

Name the cortical fissure of the human brain that forms the boundary between the

    14.   left and right hemispheres: _____ fissure

    15.   frontal and parietal lobes: _____ fissure

    16.   temporal and frontal lobes: _____ fissure

17. The major pathway of the limbic system is the _____.

18. Label the 6 structures highlighted on the following drawing of the lateral surface of the human brain.

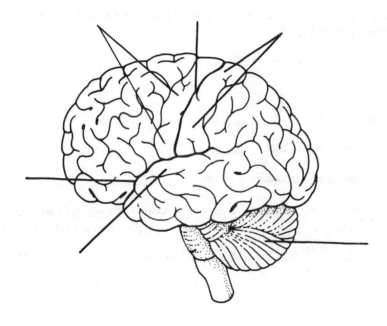

C. Short Answer Section. In no more than 4 sentences, answer each of the following questions.

1. Describe the functions of the major structures of the diencephalon.

2. Describe the difference between multipolar neurons, bipolar neurons, unipolar neurons, and interneurons.

3. Describe the shortcomings of myelin staining for the tracing of the axonal projections of individual neurons.

4. What are the two major subcortical "systems" that were described in Chapter 3? Why is it misleading to call these collections of structures "systems"?

Mark your answers to the practice examination; the correct answers follow. On the basis of your performance, plan the final stages of your studying.

Answers to Practice Examination

A. Multiple Choice Section

1. b
2. a, b, c
3. b
4. c
5. b

6. a, b, c
7. a, b
8. d
9. b, c
10. b, c

B. Modified True/False and Fill-in-the-Blank Section

1. somatic nervous system
2. spinal cord
3. autonomic nervous system
4. afferent
5. cerebral aqueduct
6. interneurons
7. dura mater; arachnoid mater; pia mater.
8. Schwann cells
9. midsagittal

10. decussate
11. F; pons and cerebellum
12. globus pallidus
13. F; mammilary bodies
14. longitudinal
15. central
16. lateral
17. fornix
18. See Figure 3.28 in BIOPSYCHOLOGY

C. Short Answer Section

1. Mention the sensory relay nuclei of the thalamus; the role of the hypothalamus in the regulation of motivated behaviors.

2. Mention the number of processes that define each class of neuron ; the fact that interneurons have little or no axon.

3. Mention that such stains cannot trace unmyelinated axons; they cannot reveal the origin or termination of individual axons; they cannot discriminate a single axon from its neighbors.

4. Mention the components of the basal ganglia and the limbic system; the uncertainty about the exact anatomy and function of these systems.

Chapter 4

NEURAL CONDUCTION AND
SYNAPTIC TRANSMISSION

I.   Jeopardy Study Items

With reference to Chapter 4 of BIOPSYCHOLOGY, write the correct answer to each of the following questions and the correct question for each of the following answers.

1. What is a membrane potential, and how is it recorded?

2.   A: -70 millivolts

3. What are the four factors that influence the distribution of
   ions on either side of a neural membrane?

4. Why is the neural membrane said to be "polarized"?

5.   A: sodium-potassium pumps

6. Postsynaptic potentials are said to be "graded"; what does
   this mean?

7. What is the difference between an EPSP and an IPSP?

8. The spread of postsynaptic potentials has two key characteristics; what are they?

9.   A: integration

10. What are the three kinds of spatial summation?

11. What are the two kinds of temporal summation?

12. Why is the spatial proximity of a synapse to the axon hillock so important?

13. What is responsible for the repolarization phase of the action potential?

14. The absolute and relative refractory periods are responsible for two important properties of neural activity. What are they?

15. The conduction of action potentials is active. What does this mean?

16.   A: at the axon hillock

17. What is the key difference between voltage-gated and chemical-gated ion channels?

18.   A: orthodromic and antidromic transmission, respectively.

19.   A: saltatory conduction

20.   A: Its main advantage is that it increases the speed of neural transmission.

21. What is the speed of axonal transmission?

22. Do action potentials occur in all neurons?

23. What are the four types of synapses?

24. What is the Golgi apparatus, and what is its function?

25. Where are peptide and nonpeptide transmitters synthesized and packaged?

26.   A: An influx of calcium ions.

27. What is exocytosis?

28. Why is it advantageous for a single neurotransmitter to have several different receptor subtypes?

29. What are the two different mechanisms by which neurotransmitters influence postsynaptic neurons?

30. What is an autoreceptor?

31.   A: the amino acid neurotransmitters, the monoamine neurotransmitters, the neuropeptides, and acetylcholine.

32.   A: Glutamate, aspartate, glycine, and GABA

33. In what way are the gas-soluble neurotransmitters different than traditional neurotransmitters?

34.   A: Dopamine, norepinephrine, and epinephrine.

35. In what sequence are the catecholamines synthesized from tyrosine?

36.   A: tryptophan

37.   A: acetylcholine

38. How is acetylcholine deactivated in the synaptic cleft?

39.   A: endorphins

40.   A: neuromodulator

41. What are agonists and antagonists?

42. Describe five ways that a drug might antagonize the effects of a neurotransmitter.

43.   A: receptor blocker.

44. How does cocaine alter the effects of the catecholamine
     neurotransmitters?

45. What are the behavioral effects of benzodiazepines?

46.   A: GABA-A receptors

47.   A: Valium and Librium, respectively.

48. How does atropine exert its effects?

49.   A: d-tubocurarine.

50.   A: muscarinic and nicotinic

Once you have completed the jeopardy study items, study them. Practice bidirectional studying; make sure
that you know the correct answer to every question and the correct question for every answer.

II.   Essay Study Questions

Using Chapter 4 of BIOPSYCHOLOGY, write an outline of the answer to each of the following essay study questions.

1. Explain the ionic basis of the resting membrane potential

2. Briefly describe the processes of temporal summation and spatial summation of postsynaptic potentials.

3. In what ways is the firing of a neuron like the firing of a gun?

4. Explain the ionic basis of the action potential.

5. Compare and contrast postsynaptic potentials and action potentials.

6. Briefly summarize the four stages of synaptic transmission: (1) synthesis and transport of the neurotransmitter, (2) release of the neurotransmitter, (3) generation of postsynaptic potentials, and (4) deactivation of the neurotransmitter.

7. Discuss the various categories of neurotransmitters and putative neurotransmitters.

8. A neurotransmitter can influence a postsynaptic neuron through either ion-channel linked or G-protein linked receptors. Compare and contrast the effect that each type of interaction has on the function of the postsynaptic neuron.

9. Describe each of the seven general steps involved in the process of synaptic transmission.

10. Compare and contrast the mechanisms of action of cocaine, the benzodiazepines, atropine, and curare.

When you have answered the essay study questions, memorize your outlines to prepare for your upcoming examination.

III. Practice Examination

After completing most of your studying of Chapter 4, but at least 24 hours before your formal examination, write the following practice examination.

A. Multiple-Choice Section. Circle the correct answer for each question; *REMEMBER that some questions may have more than one correct answer.*

1. In contrast to the classical neurotransmitters, neuropeptides are:

    a. synthesized in terminal buttons.
    b. synthesized in the cell body.
    c. released in a pulse corresponding to the arrival of each action potential.
    d. released gradually, reflecting a general increase in intracellular Ca^{++} ions.

2. Which of the following is not true?

    a. Na^+ ions leak continuously into resting neurons.
    b. K^+ ions leak continuously out of resting neurons.
    c. The pressure for Na^+ ions to move down their concentration gradient and into a resting neuron is counteracted by their electrostatic gradient.
    d. The pressure for K^+ ions to move down their concentration gradient and out of a resting neuron is partially offset by their electrostatic gradient.

3. Conduction of action potentials in myelinated axons is normally:

    a. active.
    b. passive.
    c. orthodromic.
    d. all of the above

4. In some neurons, the binding of a neurotransmitter to its receptors:

    a. opens chemically-gated ion channels.
    b. closes chemically-gated ion channels.
    c. initiates the synthesis of second messengers.
    d. all of the above

5. Axoaxonic synapses mediate:

    a. directed synapses.
    b. presynaptic inhibition.
    c. IPSPs.
    d. down regulation.

6. In some neurons, neurotransmitter is released from a series of varicosities along the axon and its branches in additional to its terminal buttons. These are:

    a. synaptic inactivation.
    b. axodendritic synapses.
    c. a directed synapse.
    d. a nondirected synapse.

7. Coexistence refers to:

    a. the situation in which two or more transmitters are found in the same terminal button.
    b. the presence of synthetic and degradative enzymes in the same terminal button.
    c. two or more presynaptic terminals forming a synapse with a single postsynaptic neuron.
    d. the degradation of a large protein into two or more neurotransmitters.

8. Which of the following is an amino acid neurotransmitter?

    a. GABA
    b. aspartate
    c. acetylcholine
    d. glutamate

9. A neuron can regulate release of its own neurotransmitter through the action of:

    a. dendritic receptors
    b. axosomatic synapses
    c. presynaptic autoreceptors
    d. IPSPs

10. Action potentials that have moved half-way down the axon cannot change direction and move back towards the axon hillock and cell body because:

    a. the ion channels only open in one direction.
    b. the action potential depletes local extracellular $Na+$ ions outside of the neuron.
    c. the area of the axon that has just participated in the action potential is in an absolute refractory period.
    d. myelin ensures that the action potential only travels in one direction.

B. Modified True-False and Fill-in-the Blank Section. If the statement is true, write TRUE in the blank provided. If the statement is false, write FALSE as well as the word or words that will make the statement true if they replaced the highlighted word or words in the original statement. If the statement is incomplete, write the word or words that will complete it.

1. True or False: The monoamine neurotransmitter that is not a catecholamine is **epinephrine.**

   A: _____

2. A _____ is a chemical transmitter that does not itself induce signals in other cells; instead, it adjusts the sensitivity of populations of cells to the excitatory or inhibitory effects of conventional neurotransmitters.

3. True or False: Motor neurons release the neurotransmitter **glutamate.**

   A: _____

4. Membrane potentials are recorded between a large _____ electrode and a thinner _____ electrode.

5. A passive property and an active property of neural membranes both contribute to the uneven distribution of ions. These are _____ and _____, respectively.

6. True or False: The key factor keeping the Na^+ ions that are outside a neuron from being driven into it by their high external concentration and the positive external charge is the **sodium/potassium pump.**

   A: _____

7. A shift in the membrane potential of a neuron from -70 to -68 mV is called a _____.

8. After an action potential, the sodium-potassium pump plays only a minor role in the restoration of the

   _____.

9. The monoamine that is not a catecholamines is called _____.

10. During an action potential, the membrane potential is depolarized to about +50 mV by the influx of

    _____ ions.

11. True or False: Vesicles are transported from the cell body to terminal buttons by **the action potential.**

    A: _____

12. True or False: The **synaptic cleft** protects neurotransmitters from degradation by cytoplasmic enzymes.

    A: _____

13. The _____ neurotransmitters are produced in the cell body and immediately diffuse through the cell membrane into the extracellular fluid to influence nearby cells.

14. The two homogenizing forces that influence the distribution of ions across the neural membrane are _____ and _____ .

15. True or False: Benzodiazepines are **antagonists** at GABAergic receptors in the nervous system.

A: _____

Which of the following terms describe postsynaptic potentials, and which describe action potentials?

16. graded   _____

17. instantaneous transmission   _____

18. integrated   _____

19. active transmission   _____

20. saltatory   _____

21. An _____ is a drug that facilitates the activity of a neurotransmitter at a synapse by enhancing its release, blocking its inactivation, or mimicking the effects of the transmitter at its receptors.

22. True or False: **Postsynaptic receptors** refer to receptors on a neuron that are activated by the same neurotransmitters that the neuron releases.

A: _____

23. True or False: Myelinated conduction of the action potential is **faster but uses more energy** than nonmyelinated conduction of the action potential.

A: _____

24. The _____ is the part of the neuron that integrates all of the excitatory and inhibitory postsynaptic potentials received by the neuron.

25. The movement of K+ ions out of a neuron would _____ the cell membrane.

C. Short Answer Section. In no more than 4 sentences, answer each of the following questions.

1. What determines whether or not a stimulated neuron will fire?

2. Describe the process of saltatory conduction and its advantages over conduction of the action potential in unmyelinated axons.

3. Describe the synthesis of epinephrine, mentioning each of the intermediate neurotransmitters that are formed.

4. Describe the release of a neurotransmitter from the terminal button.

5. Describe the G-protein linked receptors and the two ways that they can influence the postsynaptic neuron.

Mark your answers to the practice examination; the correct answers follow. On the basis of your performance, plan the final stages of your studying.

Answers to Practice Examination

A. Multiple Choice Section

1.	b; d	6.	d	
2.	c	7.	a	
3.	d	8.	a; b; d	
4.	d	9.	c	
5.	b	10.	c	

B. Modified True/False and Fill-in-the-Blank Section

1. False; serotonin
2. neuromodulator
3. False; acetylcholine
4. extracellular; intracellular
5. selective permeability of the cell membrane; the Na+/K+ pump
6. False; impermeability of the cell membrane
7. depolarization
8. distribution of ions across the cell membrane; the resting membrane potential
9. serotonin
10. Na+
11. False; microtubules
12. False; synaptic vesicles
13. soluble gas neurotransmitters
14. electrostatic pressure; random movement
15. False; agonist
16. postsynaptic potentials; action potentials
17. postsynaptic potentials; action potentials
18. postsynaptic potentials
19. action potentials
20. action potentials
21. agonist
22. False; presynaptic autoreceptors
23. False; faster and more energy efficient
24. axon hillock
25. hyperpolarize

C. Short Answer Section

1. Mention the integration of postsynaptic potentials; the threshold of activation; the axon hillock; the role of absolute and relative refractory periods.

2. Mention myelin sheaths; nodes of Ranvier; the alteration between passive and active conduction of the action potential; the increased speed of saltatory conduction.

3. Mention tyrosine; l-dopa; dopamine; norepinephrine; epinephrine.

4. Mention the arrival of the action potential at the terminal button; the influx of Ca++ ions into the terminal; synaptic vesicles; exocytosis.

5. Mention protein chains that criss-cross the cell membrane; their link to G-proteins inside cell; that G-proteins can directly elicit PSPs or act via second messengers.

Chapter 5

WHAT BIOPSYCHOLOGISTS DO:
THE RESEARCH METHODS OF BIOPSYCHOLOGY

I.   Jeopardy Study Items

With reference to Chapter 5 of BIOPSYCHOLOGY, write the correct answer to each of the following questions and the correct question for each of the following answers.

1. Prior to the early 1970s, what was one of the main impediments to biopsychological research?

2.   A: pneumoencephalography and
                                               cerebral angiography

3. What is X-ray Computed Tomography?

4. What is the key advantage of the images generated by computed tomography over conventional X-rays?

5. What brain imaging technique has even greater powers of resolution than CAT?

6.   A: It provides information about the human brain's metabolic activity.

7. How is radioactive 2-DG used in PET?

8. Describe the four advantages that Functional MRI has over PET.

9. What are the five most widely studied psychophysiological measures?

10.   A: It is a gross measure of the electrical activity of the brain.

11. What is the difference between monopolar and bipolar EEG recording?

12.   A: Sensory Evoked Potential

13. What is the purpose of signal averaging?

14.   A: Far-field potentials

15. What does EMG stand for?

16. Why is the EMG signal usually integrated?

17. What is the main correlate of increased muscle
    contraction in an EMG signal? What does it represent?

18.   A: electrooculogram

19. What is the difference between SCL and SCR?

20.   A: sweat glands

21. How does the cardiovascular system increase the flow of
    blood into particular parts of the body?

21.   A: ECG or EKG

22. What is involved in the measurement of arterial blood
    pressure?

23.   A: hypertension

24.   A: sphygmomanometer

25. What is plethysmography?

26. What is stereotaxic surgery?

27.   A: bregma

28. Describe the 4 types of lesions used in biopsychology.

29. Although cryogenic blockade produces no brain damage, it is called a functional lesion. Why?

30.   A: Elicits effects opposite that of lesions in the same area of the brain.

31. Why are most experiments utilizing intracellular unit recording techniques done in anesthetized animals?

32.   A: through skull screws rather than through scalp electrodes

33.   A: IP, IM, SC, and IV

34. Name three selective neurotoxins; what does each destroy?

35. How is the autoradiography technique different from the PET technique?

36.   A: cerebral dialysis and *in vivo* voltammetry

Chapter 5

37.   A: ligand

38. Describe the main steps of *in* situ hybridization.

39. What is a behavioral paradigm?

40. Why are neuropsychological tests normally administered?

41.   A: the WAIS

42. What are the subtests of the WAIS?

43. What is the sodium amytal test?

44. What is the dichotic listening test?

45. What is the Wisconsin Card Sorting Task? What kind of
    patient perseverates on this task?

46.   A: the token test

47.   A: the block-design subtest of the WAIS and the Rey-Osterrieth Complex Figure Test

48. What is cognitive neuroscience?

49.   A: constituent cognitive processes

50. What are *species-common* behaviors?

51.   A: thigmotaxis

52. Describe the behaviors of an alpha male rat during a typical encounter with an intruding conspecific.

53.   A: elevated plus maze

54.   A: lordosis, mount, intromission, and ejaculation

55. Describe the Pavlovian conditioning paradigm.

56. What is the difference between Pavlovian and operant conditioning?

57. Research on conditioned taste aversion challenged three
     widely held principles of learning; what were they?

58.   A: It is assessed with a radial arm maze or the Morris Maze.

59. What is the conditioned defensive burying paradigm?

60.   A: converging operations

> **Once you have completed the jeopardy study items, study them. Practice bidirectional studying; make sure that you know the correct answer to every question and the correct question for every answer.**

II.   Essay Study Questions

Using Chapter 5 of BIOPSYCHOLOGY, write an outline of the answer to each of the following essay study questions.

1. Compare and contrast conventional MRI and PET imaging techniques.

2. Explain why and how evoked potentials are averaged?

3. Compare the following kinds of electrophysiological recording: EEG recording (invasive and noninvasive), intracellular unit recording, extracellular unit recording, and multiple-unit recording.

4. Compare the different methods for producing brain lesions.

5. Describe four of the tests that a neuropsychologist would use to assess the emotional, motivational, or intellectual function of a patient suspected of suffering from impaired neural function.

6. Why are the behavioral effects of aspiration/electrolytic/radio-frequency/cryogenic brain lesions difficult to interpret? What kind of lesion technique reduces this problem?

7. What impact did the discovery of conditioned taste aversion have on theories of animal learning and the ways in which biopsychologists study animal learning in the laboratory?

8. Using any combination of the methods that you learned about in Chapter 5 of BIOPSYCHOLOGY, design an experiment that would reveal the function of prefrontal cortex.

When you have answered the essay study questions, memorize your outlines to prepare for your upcoming examination.

III. Practice Examination

After completing most of your studying of Chapter 5, but at least 24 hours before your formal examination, write the following practice examination.

A. Multiple-Choice Section. Circle the correct answer for each question; *REMEMBER that some questions may have more than one correct answer.*

1. Which of the following is a contrast X-ray technique that is used for studying the brain?

    a. angiography
    b. MRI
    c. pneumoencephalography
    d. PET

2. Which of the following is the measure of the steady level of skin conductance associated with a particular situation?

    a. SCR
    b. SCL
    c. P300
    d. ECG

3. In many stereotaxic atlases of the rat brain, one common reference point is:

    a. smegma.
    b. lambda.
    c. bregma.
    d. the tip of the nose.

4. Which of the following can be determined by extracellular unit recording?

    a. the amplitude of EPSPs and IPSPs
    b. the amplitude of APs
    c. temporal summation
    d. the rate of firing

5. The size and shape of a radio-frequency lesion is determined by:

    a. the duration and intensity of the current.
    b. the size of the subject.
    c. the configuration of the electrode
    d. the location of the electrode.

6. Which of the following can be used to destroy neurons whose cell bodies are in an area without destroying neurons whose axons are merely passing through?

    a. ibotenic acid
    b. 6-hydroxydopamine
    c. kainic acid
    d. aspiration

7. Invasive techniques used to study brain-behavior relations include:

    a. plethysmography
    b. extracellular single unit recording
    c. *in vivo* microdialysis
    d. functional MRI

8. In stereotaxic surgery, the electrode is:

    a. positioned relative to some consistent landmark or reference point.
    b. guided using a stereotaxic head holder.
    c. usually placed on the surface of the brain.
    d. usually implanted directly into the brain.

9. The major objectives of behavioral research methods are to:

    a. produce the behavior under study and then objectively measure it.
    b. control, simplify, and objectify behavior.
    c. eliminate undesirable behaviors from the subject under study.
    d. understand the underlying neural bases of behaviors.

10. The paired-image subtraction technique involves:

    a. obtaining CAT images from several different subjects.
    b. subtracting PET or MRI images generated during one task from images generated during another.
    c. examining differences between far-field potentials.
    d. combining differences in electrical activity recorded between the front and back of the eye.

B. Modified True-False and Fill-in-the Blank Section. If the statement is true, write TRUE in the blank provided. If the statement is false, write FALSE as well as the word or words that will make the statement true if they replaced the highlighted word or words in the original statement. If the statement is incomplete, write the word or words that will complete it.

1. True or False: **Cerebral angiography** has higher powers of resolution than CAT.

    A: _____

2. Unlike CAT and MRI scans, _____ scans provide information about the metabolic activity of the brain.

What do the following abbreviations stand for?

3. PET: _____

4. MRI: _____

5. CAT: _____

6. In humans, EEG electrodes are usually placed on the _____.

7. True or False: In **bipolar EEG recording**, one electrode is attached on the target site and the other is attached to a point of relative electrical silence such as the ear lobe.

    A: _____

8. In EEG recording, alpha waves are associated with _____.

9. True or False: The electrophysiological technique for recording eye movements is called **electromyography**.

    A: _____

10. Because the cardiovascular system is not a single _____ loop, blood can be directed to various parts of the body by constriction of particular _____ muscles in the walls of arterioles.

11. "Plethysmos" is Greek for "an _____."

12. _____ involves the placement of an electrode or some other device at a specific target site in the brain.

13. Reversible lesions of neural tissue can be accomplished using _____ blockade or by injecting _____ directly into the brain.

14. The sodium amytal test is a test of language _____.

Chapter 5

Which lesion technique would most likely be used to make permanent lesions to each of the following structures?

15.   a large area of frontal cortex: _____

16.   optic nerve: _____

17.   hypothalamus: _____

18.   True or False: **Extracellular single-unit recording techniques** allow a researcher to record the electrical activity of single neurons in a freely-moving animal.

           A: _____

19.   The location of a particular neurotransmitter in the brain can be determined using techniques such as _____ or _____.

20.   A set of procedures developed for the investigation of a particular behavioral phenomenon is commonly referred to as a _____.

21.   There are two categories of subtests in the WAIS; these are the performance subtests and the _____ subtests.

22.   The _____ test is a brief screening test of language ability.

23.   True or False: The **token test** subtest of the WAIS is commonly used to assess 3-dimensional complex visuospatial ability?

           A: _____

24.   Patients with frontal-lobe lesions often display perseveration on the _____ Sorting Test.

25.   Behaviors that are displayed by virtually all members of a species that are the same age and sex are called _____ behaviors.

26.   In the open-field test, the lack of activity, thigmotaxis, and the number of _____ that are dropped are commonly employed measures of fearfulness.

What would each of the following be used to study?

27.   open field: _____

28.   self-administration box: _____

29.   radial-arm maze: _____

30.   Morris water maze: _____

Which behavioral paradigms have been used to study the following?

31. The defensive behaviors rats direct at inanimate objects: the conditioned defensive
_____ paradigm

32. The rewarding effects of brain stimulation: the_____ paradigm

33. The learning of associations between tastes and illness: the conditioned _____
paradigm

34. Rats and many other animals are _____; that is, they are fearful of
new objects in their environment.

35. Rats with bilateral _____ lesions are hyperreactive to an experimenter
when they are handled.

C. Short Answer Section. In no more than 4 sentences, answer each of the following questions.

1. Compare and contrast the techniques of *in vivo voltammetry* and *in vivo microdialysis.*

2. Why are imaging techniques like PET or MRI more useful than standard X-ray photographs in studying the
brain?

3. Biopsychological research often involves a variety of recording, stimulation, neurochemical, lesion, and imaging
techniques; why are a variety of techniques so often necessary to understand brain-behavior relations?

Mark your answers to the practice examination; the correct answers follow. On the basis of your
performance, plan the final stages of your studying.

Answers to Practice Examination

A. Multiple Choice Section

1. a, c
2. a
3. c
4. d
5. a, c

6. a, c
7. b, c
8. a, d
9. a, b
10. b

B. Modified True/False and Fill-in-the-Blank Section

1. F; magnetic resonance imaging
2. PET
3. Positron Emission Tomography
4. Magnetic Resonance Imaging
5. Computerized Axial Tomography
6. scalp
7. F; monopolar
8. relaxed wakefulness
9. F; electrooculography
10. closed; sphincter
11. enlargement
12. Stereotaxic surgery
13. cryogenic; local anesthetics
14. laterality
15. aspiration
16. knife cuts
17. radio-frequency
18. True

19. immunocytochemistry; *in situ* hybridization
20. behavioral paradigm
21. verbal substests (see Table 5.1)
22. token
23. F; block-design subtest
24. Wisconsin Card
25. species-common
26. fecal boluses
27. fear
28. role of conditioning in drug taking behaviors
29. the spatial abilities of rodents
30. the spatial abilities of rodents
31. burying
32. self-stimulation
33. taste-aversion
34. neophobic
35. septal

C. Short Answer Section

1. Mention that both are invasive techniques; that microdialysis measures neurochemicals in the brain whereas extracellular single-unit recordings measure the electrical activity of neurons in the brain; mention that both techniques can be used in freely-moving animals.

2. Mention the increased resolution of PET and MRI; mention the ability to image the brain in behaving subjects with PET and MRI.

3. Mention that each technique has unique strengths and shortcomings; the need for converging operations.

Chapter 6

HUMAN BRAIN DAMAGE AND ANIMAL MODELS

I.   Jeopardy Study Items

With reference to Chapter 6 of BIOPSYCHOLOGY, write the correct answer to each of the following questions and the correct question for each of the following answers.

1. What are meningiomas?

2. What is the difference between a benign tumor and a malignant tumor?

3.   A: encapsulated tumors

4.   A: infiltrating tumors

5.   A: metastatic tumors

75

6. What is a tumor suppressor gene?

7. What is an aneurysm?

8.   A: intracerebral hemorrhage and cerebral ischemia

9.   A: stroke

10. What are the 3 main causes of stroke?

11. What is the difference between a thrombus and an embolus?

12. Which neurotransmitter is thought to play a key role in stroke-related brain damage?

13.   A: a subdural hematoma

14. What is a contre coup injury?

15. What is the difference between a contusion and a concussion?

16.   A: the punch-drunk syndrome

17. What is encephalitis?

18. What is meningitis?

19.   A: the syndrome of insanity and dementia resulting from syphilitic infection

20. What is the difference between a neurotropic and a pantropic viral infection?

21.   A: the mumps and herpes

22. What is a toxic psychosis?

23.   A: "mad as a hatter"

24.   A: "crackpot"

25. What is tardive dyskinesia?

26. What is the difference between exogenous and endogenous neurotoxins?

27. Which genetic abnormality is associated with Down's syndrome?

28. What are the symptoms of Down's syndrome?

29. Why are genetic abnormalities rarely associated with dominant genes?

33. What is unusual about the gene that underlies the development of Huntington's disease?

30. Why is the differential diagnosis of patients suffering from neuropsychological dysfunction often so difficult?

31.   A: epilepsy

32. What is the difference between a seizure and a convulsion?

33. What is an epileptic aura? Why are they important in the diagnosis and management of epilepsy?

34.   A: generalized seizures and partial seizures

35. Why is epilepsy considered to be a number of different,
     though related, diseases?

36. What is the difference between a simple partial seizure
     and a complex partial seizure?

37.   A: a psychomotor attack

38. How do generalized seizures begin?

39. What are the differences between grand mal and petit mal
     seizures?

40. Describe the symptoms of a grand mal seizure.

41.   A: petit mal absence

42. What are the major symptoms of Parkinson's disease?

43.   A: damage to dopaminergic neurons that project from the
                                       substantia nigra to the striatum

44. What is l-dopa?

45. What is unusual about the genetic basis of Huntington's disease?

46. What are the symptoms of Huntington's disease?

47.   A: general shrinkage of the brain and degeneration of the striatum and cerebral cortex

48. Describe the neuropathology that underlies multiple sclerosis?

49. What are the symptoms of multiple sclerosis?

50.   A: the study of various factors that influence the distribution of disease in the general population.

51.   A: experimental allergic encephalomyelitis

52. What is the incidence of Alzheimer's disease?

53. What are the symptoms of Alzheimer's disease?

54.   A: neurofibrillary tangles and amyloid plaques

55. What is the relation between Down's syndrome and
    Alzheimer's disease?

56. What evidence suggests that Alzheimer's disease is not a
    unitary disorder?

57.   A: a homologous animal model

58. What kind of animal model resembles a human disorder,
    but is artificially produced in the laboratory?

59.   A: a predictive animal model

60. Why must the results of research employing animal
    models by interpreted with caution?

61. What is kindling?

62.   In what ways is kindling a general   phenomenon?

63.   A: the underlying neural changes are permanent, and massed
                                             stimulations will not produce it

64.   In what two ways does kindling model epilepsy?

65.   How is a syndrome of spontaneous kindled convulsions induced?

66.   A: amphetamine psychosis

67.   What evidence links amphetamine psychosis and schizophrenia?

68.   A: behavioral stereotypies

69.   A: MPTP

70.   What evidence has linked MPTP poisoning to Parkinson's disease?

71.   A: deprenyl

72.   A: monoamine oxidase

Once you have completed the jeopardy study items, study them. Practice bidirectional studying; make sure that you know the correct answer to every question and the correct question for every answer.

II.   Essay Study Questions

Using Chapter 6 of BIOPSYCHOLOGY, write an outline of the answer to each of the following essay study questions.

1. Describe the role that glutamate plays in the development of stroke-induced brain damage.

2. The more that is known about the causes and neural bases of a neuropsychological disorder, the more accurately it can be diagnosed; the more accurately it can be diagnosed, the more readily its causes and neural bases can be identified. Explain.

3. What is the evidence that amphetamine-produced locomotion, but not oral stereotypy, models amphetamine psychosis?

4. Describe the major categories of epilepsy.

5. Parkinson's disease, Huntington's disease, and multiple sclerosis are movement disorders; compare and contrast these diseases.

6. Describe the behavioral and neuropathological symptoms of Alzheimer's disease. What evidence suggests that it has a genetic basis?

7. Compare homologous, isomorphic, and predictive animal models and their role in biopsychological research

8. Describe and discuss the kindling model of epilepsy.

When you have answered the essay study questions, memorize your outlines to prepare for your upcoming examination.

III.   Practice Examination

After completing most of your studying of Chapter 6, but at least 24 hours before your formal examination, write the following practice examination.

A. Multiple-Choice Section. Circle the correct answer for each question; *REMEMBER that some questions may have more than one correct answer.*

1.   Meningiomas:

     a. grow between the meninges.
     b. are usually benign.
     c. are usually metastatic.
     d. all of the above

2. Infiltrating tumors are usually:

    a. meningiomas.
    b. benign.
    c. malignant.
    d. both a and b

3. Which neuropsychological disorders have a strong genetic component?

    a. Huntington's disease
    b. Parkinson's disease
    c. Alzheimer's disease
    d. epilepsy

4. General paresis is:

    a. an officer in the Spanish army.
    b. caused by a viral infection.
    c. caused by a bacterial infection.
    d. caused by the syphilis bacteria.

5. The mumps and herpes viruses are:

    a. pantropic infections.
    b. neurotropic infections.
    c. bacterial infections.
    d. both a and c

6. Tardive dyskinesia is produced by:

    a. meningitis.
    b. antipsychotic drugs.
    c. bacterial infection.
    d. syphilis.

7. Which kind of animal model has the same etiology (cause) as the human disorder that it is modeling?

    a. a homologous model
    b. an isomorphic model
    c. a predictive model
    d. a plastic model

8. Kindled convulsions have been produced:

    a. in primates.
    b. by drugs.
    c. by amygdala stimulation.
    d. by hippocampus stimulation.

9. The development of multiple sclerosis is influenced by:

    a. depletion of the neurotransmitter dopamine.
    b. environmental factors, as people raised in cool climates are more likely to develop the disease.
    c. environmental factors, as people raised in warm climates are more likely to develop the disease.
    d. genetic factors.

10. Which of the following drugs are identified neurotoxins?

    a. lead
    b. mercury
    c. MPTP
    d. alcohol

B. Modified True-False and Fill-in-the Blank Section. If the statement is true, write TRUE in the blank provided. If the statement is false, write FALSE as well as the word or words that will make the statement true if they replaced the highlighted word or words in the original statement. If the statement is incomplete, write the word or words that will complete it.

1. The effects of many minor concussions can accumulate to produce a serious disorder called the
   _____ syndrome.

2. True or False: **Embolism** in blood vessel walls are a common cause of intracerebral hemorrhage.

   A: _____

3. The first recorded case of _____ was reported in the town of Bures, England in 1630.

4. A schizophrenia-like syndrome can be induced in humans who abuse _____,
   cocaine, or other _____ drugs.

5. A contusion is a closed head injury that results in a _____, or bruise, which often accumulates in the subdural space.

6. True or False: Kindling is most rapidly produced by **massed stimulations** of the amygdala or hippocampus.

   A: _____

7. A parkinsonian syndrome can be induced in humans and other primates with injections of _____.

Fill in each of the following blanks with the name of the related neurological disorder: epilepsy, Parkinson's disease, Huntington's disease, multiple sclerosis, or Alzheimer's disease.

8. neurofibrillary tangles: _____

9. chromosome 21: _____

10. experimental allergic encephalomyelitis: _____

11. auras: _____

12. nigrostriatal pathway: _____

13. psychomotor attack: _____

14. choreiform movement: _____

15. autoimmune disease: _____

16. True or False: The observation of a **grand mal** seizure is incontrovertible evidence of epilepsy.

    A: _____

17. Much of the brain damage associated with stroke is a consequence of the excessive release of the neurotransmitter _____.

C. Short Answer Section. In no more than 4 sentences, answer each of the following questions.

1. Why have recently developed genetic tests placed the offspring of parents who develop Huntington's disease in a difficult situation?

2. Describe the symptoms and neuropathology of Parkinson's disease.

3. Compare and contrast the different kinds of cerebrovascular disorders.

Mark your answers to the practice examination; the correct answers follow.   On the basis of your performance, plan the final stages of your studying.

Answers to Practice Examination

A. Multiple Choice Section

1. a, b
2. c
3. a, c
4. d
5. a

6. b
7. a
8. a, b, c, d
9. b, d
10. a, b, c, d

B. Modified True/False and Fill-in-the-Blank Section

1. punch-drunk
2. F; Aneurysms
3. Huntington's disease
4. amphetamine; psychostimulant
5. hematoma
6. F; distributed
7. MPTP
8. Alzheimer's disease
9. Alzheimer's disease
10. multiple sclerosis
11. epilepsy
12. Parkinson's disease
13. epilepsy
14. Huntington's disease
15. multiple sclerosis
16. F; spontaneous epileptic discharges in the EEG
17. glutamate

C. Short Answer Section

1. Mention the screen allows offspring to know whether they carry the gene for Huntington's disease; that this gene is dominant, meaning that they will undoubtedly develop the disease as they grow older; that they will also have a 50/50 chance of passing it on to their offspring.

2. Mention the stiffness, tremor, inactivity, slowness of movement, difficulty initiating movement, mask-like face, seborrhea and micrographia; that the disease is due to destruction of dopaminergic neurons in the substantia nigra that project to the striatum.

3. Mention intracerebral hemorrhage and stroke; that intracerebral hemorrhage is actual intracranial bleeding that is often due to aneurysms, while stroke is brain damage due to obstruction of cerebral vasculature due to thrombosis, embolism, or arteriosclerosis.

Chapter 7

THE VISUAL SYSTEM: FROM EYE TO CORTEX

I.   Jeopardy Study Items

With reference to Chapter 7 of BIOPSYCHOLOGY, write the correct answer to each of the following questions and the correct question for each of the following answers.

1. Describe the "dual-identity" of light.

2.   A: electromagnetic energy between 380 and 760 nanometers.

3. What are the psychological correlates of wavelength and
      intensity?

4. It is said that the adjustment of pupil size in response to
      changes in illumination represents a compromise between
      acuity and sensitivity. What does this mean?

5.   A: focuses light on the retina

6.   A: accommodation

7. Why do some animals have their eyes mounted side-by-side on the front of their heads?

8. How does the degree of binocular disparity provide a basis for seeing in three dimensions?

9.   A: receptors, horizontal cells, bipolar cells, amacrine cells, retinal ganglion cells

10. What is responsible for the blind spot in everybody's visual field?

11.   A: fovea

12. What is visual completion?

13.   A: surface interpolation

14.   A: photopic vision

15. What is scotopic vision?

16. The photopic and scotopic systems differ markedly in convergence. What are the consequences of this difference?

17. How are rods and cones distributed over the retina?

18.   A: nasal hemiretina

19.   A: a spectral sensitivity curve

20. What is the difference between the photopic and scotopic spectral sensitivity curves?

21. What is the Purkinje effect, and why does it occur?

22.   A: saccades

23.   A: temporal integration

24. What does stabilized image research suggest about the function of eye movement?

25.   A: transduction

26.   A: rhodopsin

27. What evidence is there that absorption of light by rhodopsin is the first, critical step in the process of vision?

28. How does light affect rhodopsin?

29. How does light alter the membrane potential of
     rhodopsin receptors?

30. How does visual input from the left and right hemiretinas
     of each eye reach the primary visual cortex?

31.   A: retinotopic

32. What is the functional significance of the optic chiasm?

33.   A: it conveys visual information about color, fine pattern
                                       details, and slow or stationary object.

34.   A: an edge

35.   A: Mach bands

36. What is lateral inhibition? Explain how it results in
     contrast enhancement?

37. What is a receptive field?

38. How do Hubel and Wiesel study visual system neurons?

39.   A: lower layer IV

40. Which levels of the retina-geniculate- striate visual
     system have round receptive fields?

41. What is "on firing" and "off firing"?

42.   A: on-center cells and off-center cells

43. What evidence suggests that many cells in the retina-
     geniculate-striate system respond best to contrast?

44.   A: simple cells and complex cells

45. What are the main features of the receptive fields of
     simple cortical cells?

46. What are the main features of the receptive fields of
     complex cortical cells?

47.   A: virtually all of them are monocular

48.   A: over half of them display ocular dominance

49. What accounts for the characteristic receptive fields of
    the cells in visual cortex?

50. What is an aggregate field?

51. What is the evidence for columnar organization of
    receptive field location in visual cortex?

52. What experimental results suggest that the input into
    lower layer IV from each eye occurs in alternating
    stripes?

53.   A: sine-wave grating

54. What are the two key principles that underlie the spatial-
    frequency theory of visual cortex function?

55. What produces our perception of the achromatic colors?

56. What determines our perception of an object's color?

57. What is the component theory of color vision?

58. What is the opponent theory of color vision?

59.   A: complementary colors

60. How is a complementary afterimage formed?

61.   A: microspectrophotometry

62. What evidence suggests that there are three different kinds of cones?

63. What evidence suggests that visual system neurons respond to different wavelengths according to opponent principles?

64. What is the major advantage of color constancy in the visual system?

65. Describe Land's retinex theory of color vision.

66. What are dual-opponent color cells?

67.   A: cytochrome oxidase blobs

68. In the parlance of a neuroscientist, what are blobs?

Once you have completed the jeopardy study items, study them. Practice bidirectional studying; make sure that you know the correct answer to every question and the correct question for every answer.

II.   Essay Study Questions

Using Chapter 7 of BIOPSYCHOLOGY, write an outline of the answer to each of the following essay study questions.

1. Describe the function of the ocular factors that influence the nature of the retinal image.

2. Describe the anatomical and functional characteristics of the two channels of the retina-geniculate-striate system.

3. How did Land (1977) demonstrate color constancy?

4. What is the duplexity theory of vision? Describe the evidence that supports it.

5. What are the photopic and scotopic spectral sensitivity curves? Draw them and then explain the Purkinje effect by referring to your drawing.

6. Describe the importance of eye movements to the function of the visual system.

7. Draw the retina-geniculate-striate system. With reference to it, explain the paths followed by signals from the left and right eyes. The layout of the visual system is retinotopic; what does this mean?

8. By referring to a schematic drawing of Limulus ommatidia, explain how mutual inhibition results in contrast enhancement.

9. Compare the receptive fields of complex cells, simple cells, and the neurons in lower layer IV of visual cortex.

10. Describe Hubel and Wiesel's model of visual cortex organization and the experimental results on which this model is based.

When you have answered the essay study questions, memorize your outlines to prepare for your upcoming examination.

III.   Practice Examination

After completing most of your studying of Chapter 7, but at least 24 hours before your formal examination, write the following practice examination.

A. Multiple-Choice Section. Circle the correct answer for each question; *REMEMBER that some questions may have more than one correct answer.*

1. Humans can see electromagnetic waves of energy that have a length of:

    a. 40 to 90 nanometers.
    b. 380 to 760 nanometers.
    c. 1,000 to 4,000 nanometers.
    d. 260 to 380 nanometers.

2. The psychological correlates of wavelength and intensity are:

    a. color and brightness, respectively.
    b. brightness and hue, respectively.
    c. shape and color, respectively.
    d. brightness and shape, respectively.

3. The adjustment of pupil size in response to changes in illumination represents a compromise between:

    a. size and position.
    b. color and intensity.
    c. sensitivity and acuity.
    d. color and shape.

4. When rhodopsin is moved from the dark to intense light,

    a. it absorbs light in the same range of wavelengths as the scotopic spectral sensitivity curve.
    b. it starts to become bleached.
    c. it becomes an intense red color.
    d. it gains light-absorbing properties.

5. The photopic visual system is characterized by:

    a. a high degree of convergence onto bipolar cells.
    b. maximal sensitivity to light in the range of 560 nanometers.
    c. high visual acuity.
    d. high sensitivity.

6. Off-center cells include:

    a. rods and cones.
    b. retinal ganglion cells.
    c. simple cortical cells.
    d. complex cortical cells.

7. Hubel and Wiesel injected a radioactive amino acid into one eye of their subjects, and then later they subjected slices of the subjects' striate cortex to autoradiography. They observed:

    a. alternating patches of radioactivity and nonradioactivity in all cortical layers.
    b. radioactivity in only one hemisphere.
    c. alternating patches of radioactivity and nonradioactivity in lower layer IV.
    d. orientation specificity.

8. The spatial-frequency theory of visual cortex function is based on the principle that any:

    a. visual array can be represented by plotting the intensity of light along lines running through it.
    b. curve can be broken down into constituent sine waves by Fourier analysis.
    c. sine-wave grating is orientation free.
    d. visual cell is more sensitive to a simple bar of light than a sine-wave grating.

9. Because of the phenomenon of color constancy, the color of an object:

    a. varies with changes in illumination.
    b. does not vary, even though there may be major changes in the wavelengths of light that it reflects.
    c. will vary depending on whether the photopic or the scotopic visual system is active.
    d. does not vary regardless of whether the photopic or the scotopic visual system is active.

10. The retinal ganglion cells:

    a. are responsible for scotopic vision.
    b. release the excitatory neurotransmitter glutamate.
    c. transduce light energy in the range of 560 nanometers.
    d. are the most superficial layer of cells in the retina.

11. The retina-geniculate-striate system:

    a. contains neurons that are generally monocular.
    b. is retinotopically organized.
    c. includes ommitidia and the lateral plexus.
    d. conveys information from each eye to primary visual cortex in both hemispheres.

12. Cones are to rods as:

    a. color vision is to viewing shades of gray.
    b. photopic vision is to scotopic vision.
    c. high sensitivity is to high acuity.
    d. high convergence is to low convergence.

13. The M pathway for visual information is:

    a. responsible for conveying information about slowly moving objects.
    b. comprised of magnocellular neurons in the lateral geniculate and the retinal ganglion cells that project on them.
    c. largely responsible from conveying information from rod receptors.
    d. found in the upper four layers of the lateral geniculate nucleus of the thalamus.

B. Modified True-False and Fill-in-the Blank Section. If the statement is true, write TRUE in the blank provided. If the statement is false, write FALSE as well as the word or words that will make the statement true if they replaced the highlighted word or words in the original statement. If the statement is incomplete, write the word or words that will complete it.

1. True or False: Retinal ganglion cell axons from the **temporal hemiretinas** decussate to synapse in the lateral geniculate nucleus of the thalamus in the contralateral hemisphere.

    A: _____

2. Signals from an object viewed in the left visual field are projected to striate cortex in the _____ hemisphere.

3. At the boundary between two adjacent areas that differ in intensity, the more intense area looks even more intense than it really is, and the less intense area looks even less intense than it really is. This accentuation of edges is called _____ enhancement.

4. The "preferred" type of stimulus for most neurons of the striate cortex is a _____.

5. A _____ is sufficient to elicit the firing of simple cells but not complex cells.

6. About half the complex cortical cells are _____, and over half of these display some degree of ocular _____.

7. True or False: The area covered by the receptive fields of all of the cells in a particular column of striate cortex is called the **receptive field** of that column.

    A: _____

8. Microspectrophotometry experiments have confirmed the prediction of the _____ theory of color vision.

9. True or False: When an ommitidia receptor fires, it inhibits the activity of its neighbors because of the inhibitory interconnections of **bipolar cells.**

    A: _____

10. The discovery of dual-opponent color cells provided a means of explaining the physiological basis of color _____.

11. Dual-opponent color cells have particularly high concentrations of _____.

12. Light can be thought of in two different ways: as discrete particles called _____, or as _____ of electromagnetic energy.

13. After a few seconds of viewing, a simple _____ disappears, leaving a featureless gray field.

14. Svaetichin (1956) discovery that retinal neurons responded in one direction (e.g., hyperpolarization or depolarization) to blue and in the other direction to yellow confirmed the prediction of the _____ theory of color vision.

15. According to the Nobel-Prize winning research of Hubel and Wiesel, primary visual cortex neurons are grouped in functional _____.

16. True or False: Virtually all of the neurons in the **retina-geniculate-striate pathway** are monocular.

    A: _____

17. According to the _____ theory of color vision, the color of a particular stimulus is encoded by the ratio of three different kinds of color receptors.

18. True or False: The high acuity of cone receptors in the retina is due to their **high degree of convergence** onto retinal ganglion cells.

    A: _____

19. When radioactive 2-DG is injected into a single eye, it produces alternating patches of radioactivity in _____, reflecting the pattern of inputs from each eye.

20. True or False: The **P pathway** conveys information about movement through the retina-geniculate-striate pathway.

    A: _____

21. Severing the optic chiasm along the midsagittal plane would produce blindness in the visual fields for the _____ hemiretinas of each eye.

22. The perception of an edge is really the perception of a _____ between two adjacent areas of the visual field.

23. According to the opponent-process theory of color vision, the color of a particular stimulus is encoded by two classes of color-sensitive cells that encode _____ color perceptions (e.g., blue and yellow).

24. The visual system uses information provided by receptors around your blind spot to fill in the gaps in your retinal image; this phenomenon is called _____.

25. True or False: At night, the Purkinje effect is evident because yellow flowers appear as a **brighter shade** of gray than blue flowers.

    A: _____

26. A graph of the relative brightness of lights of the same intensity presented at different wavelengths is called a _____.

27. Your eyes move around their visual fields about three times every second; these movements are called _____.

C. Short Answer Section. In no more than 4 sentences, answer each of the following questions.

1. Describe the spatial-frequency theory of vision.

2. Define the component and opponent theories of color vision.

3. What is color constancy? In what respect does color constancy create a problem for the component and opponent theories?

4. Label the six different types of cells that are presented in the following diagram of the mammalian retina.

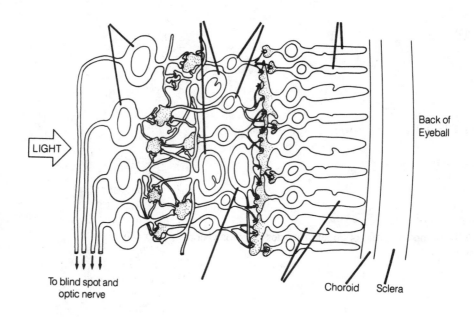

LIGHT

Back of
Eyeball

To blind spot and
optic nerve

Choroid   Sclera

5. Label 10 structures in the following drawing of the human eye.

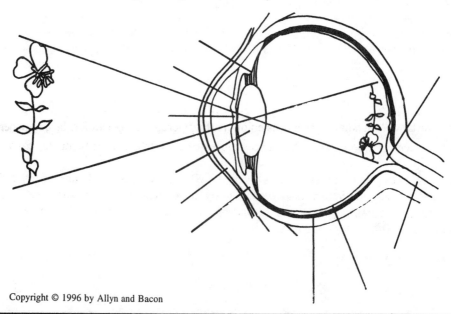

Mark your answers to the practice examination; the correct answers follow. On the basis of your performance, plan the final stages of your studying.

Answers to Practice Examination

A. Multiple Choice Section

1. b
2. a
3. c
4. a, b
5. b, c
6. b
7. c

8. a, b
9. b
10. b, d
11. a, b, d
12. a, b
13. b, c

B. Modified True/False and Fill-in-the-Blank Section

1. F; nasal hemiretina
2. contralateral
3. contrast
4. dot of light
5. stationary bar of light
6. binocular, dominance
7. F; aggregate field
8. component process
9. the lateral plexus
10. constancy
11. cytochrome oxidase
12. photons; waves
13. stationary stimulus
14. opponent-process

15. columns
16. True
17. component-process
18. F; low degree of convergence
19. primary visual cortex
20. F; M pathway
21. nasal
22. contrast
23. complementary
24. completion
25. F; darker
26. spectral sensitivity curve
27. saccades

C. Short Answer Section

1. Mention the physical principles that stimuli can be represented a plots of the light intensity along lines running through the stimulus and that any curve can be broken down into constituent sine waves; that each module of visual cortex responds selectively to specific frequencies and orientations of sine-wave gratings; that perception is a summation of the action of all cortical modules that are activated by a visual stimulus.

2. Mention component processing as color perception reflecting the ratio of activity at three different color receptors; opponent processing as color perception reflecting the activity of two different classes of receptors encoding complementary colors; mention that both processes are active in the mammalian visual system.

3. Mention that color perception is constant even when different wavelengths of light are reflected; that color perception is a function of the comparison of a stimulus with adjacent areas in the visual field; that this cannot be accounted for by component process and opponent process theories, which suggest that perception is a function of the wavelength of reflected light.

4. See Figure 7.4 in BIOPSYCHOLOGY.

5. See Figure 7.2 in BIOPSYCHOLOGY.

Chapter 8

MECHANISMS OF PERCEPTION

I.   Jeopardy Study Items

With reference to Chapter 8 of BIOPSYCHOLOGY, write the correct answer to each of the following questions and the correct question for each of the following answers.

1.   A: vision, touch, hearing, olfaction, and taste

2. What is the difference between primary and secondary sensory cortex?? Between sensory cortex and association cortex??

3. What is a hierarchical system?

4. What is the traditional, hierarchical model of sensory system organization?

5. Describe the general pattern of deficits that emerges from damage to progressively higher levels of any sensory system.

6. What is the difference between sensation and perception?

7.   A: functional segregation

8. What is the difference between serial processing and
   parallel processing?

9.   A: prestriate cortex and inferotemporal cortex

10.   A: a scotoma

11. Describe the perimetry test.

12. What is blind-sight?

13.   A: subjective contours

14.   A: posterior parietal cortex

15. What is visual agnosia?

16. What evidence suggests that the perceptual deficits of
    prosopagnosics are not restricted to the perception of
    faces?

17.   A: the inferior prestriate area and adjacent portions of
                                         inferotemporal cortex

18. What is sound?

19.   A: they determine loudness, pitch, and timbre, respectively

20. What is the difference between the ear drum and the oval window?

21.   A: incus, malleus, and stapes

22. How is sound transduced in the organ of Corti?

23.   A: tonotopic

24. What is the function of the semicircular canals?

25.   A: medial geniculate nuclei of the thalamus

26. What two kinds of information are used to localize sounds in space?

27.   A: barn owls

28. What are the effects of auditory cortex damage?

29.   A: word deafness

30. What are the three divisions of the somatosensory
     system?

31.   A: the system for perceiving mechanical stimuli, thermal
                                                 stimuli, and nociceptive stimuli

32. What are the four types of cutaneous receptors?

33.   A: it is mediated by free nerve endings

34.   A: stereognosis

35. What is a dermatome?

36. Describe the dorsal-column medial-lemniscus system
     pathway.

37.   A: it carries information to the cortex about pain and
                                                 temperature

38.   A: the dorsal column neurons originating in the toes

39. What are S1 and S2?

40. What are the three tracts of the anterolateral system?

41.   A: the trigeminal nerve

42.   A: parafascicular and intralaminar nuclei of the thalamus

43. Describe the location and organization of primary
    somatosensory cortex.

44.   A: hands, lips, and tongue

45. What is the effect of somatosensory cortex damage in
    humans?

46.   A: asomatognosia

47. Extensive damage to the right posterior parietal lobe is
    associated with three neuropsychological deficits;
    describe each of these.

48. What area of the cortex mediates the perception of pain?

49.   A: anterior cingulate cortex

50.   A: gate-control theory

51. Describe the periaqueductal gray and its role in the
    perception of pain.

52. What are endorphins?

53. What is the PAG-raphé-dorsal-column analgesia circuit?

54. What is phantom-limb pain?

55.   A: chemical senses

56.   What is flavor?

57.   What are pheromones?

58. What evidence is there that humans release sex
    pheromones?

59.   A: cribriform plate

60. What circuits carry olfactory information into the cerebral hemispheres?

61. Describe the neural circuitry of the olfactory system.

62. What is unique about the way that olfactory information reaches the cortex?

63.   A: orbitofrontal cortex

64. What are the primary tastes?

65.   A: the facial, vagus, and glossopharyngeal cranial nerves

66. How do the gustatory projections differ from those of the other sensory systems?

67. What is anosmia? How is it usually caused?

68. What is ageusia? What can sometimes cause ageusia for the anterior two-thirds of the tongue?

69.   A: selective attention

70.   What effect does selective attention have on cell firing
       and perception?

Once you have completed the jeopardy study items, study them. Practice bidirectional studying; make sure that you know the correct answer to every question and the correct question for every answer.

II.   Essay Study Questions

Using Chapter 8 of BIOPSYCHOLOGY, write an outline of the answer to each of the following essay study questions.

1.   Describe the dorsal and ventral pathways by which information leaves visual cortex and the type of information
      that is conveyed by each one.

2.   Draw and label the key structures of the ear. By referring to your drawing, describe the transduction of sound
      waves into auditory sensations.

3. Describe the organization and function of the three subdivisions of the exteroceptive branch of the somatosensory system.

4. Describe the transmission of touch-pressure information through the dorsal-column medial-lemniscus system.

5. Describe two paradoxes of pain.

6. Draw the descending circuit has been hypothesized to mediate analgesia. Describe the evidence supporting this model.

7. Label the anterolateral pathway, the dorsal columns, the PAG, and the raphé in the following drawing of the hypothetical descending analgesia circuit; describe the function of this circuit.

8. Describe the hierarchical organization of the visual system, from the retina to areas of association cortex.

9. Your friend was injured in a car accident and suffered extensive and irreparable damage to their primary visual cortex. However, you note that they still react to some visual stimuli; to what would you attribute this visual capacity? Describe the characteristics of this auxiliary visual system.

10. Compare and contrast the function of the olfactory system and the visual system.

> **When you have answered the essay study questions, memorize your outlines to prepare for your upcoming examination.**

III. Practice Examination

> *After completing most of your studying of Chapter 8, but at least 24 hours before your formal examination, write the following practice examination.*

A. Multiple-Choice Section. Circle the correct answer for each question; *REMEMBER that some questions may have more than one correct answer.*

1. The flow of information in visual cortex goes from:

    a. primary visual cortex to prestriate cortex.
    b. prestriate cortex to posterior parietal cortex.
    c. prestriate cortex to inferotemporal cortex.
    d. posterior parietal cortex to inferotemporal cortex.

2. Much auditory cortex is in the depths of the:

    a. central fissure.
    b. lateral fissure.
    c. longitudinal fissure.
    d. occipital fissure.

3. Patients with auditory cortex lesions have difficulty:

    a. recognizing simple auditory stimuli.
    b. understanding rapid speech.
    c. judging the temporal order of sounds presented in rapid succession.
    d. listening to sounds of long duration.

4. There are many opiate receptors in the:

    a. dorsal horns.
    b. anterolateral system.
    c. PAG.
    d. raphé nucleus.

5. The neurons of the raphé are:

    a. cholinergic.
    b. serotonergic.
    c. adrenergic.
    d. dopaminergic.

6. The organ of Corti:

    a. contains the hair cells that transduce sound waves into sensation.
    b. is composed of the basilar membrane and the tympanic membrane.
    c. lies in the middle ear.
    d. carries information from the anterior two-thirds of the ipsilateral half of the tongue.

7. The dorsal pathway for projections from primary visual cortex:

    a. is responsible for conveying "what" information to inferotemporal cortex.
    b. conveys information received largely from the M-pathway alone.
    c. projects to dorsal prestriate cortex and then to inferotemporal cortex.
    d. projects to dorsal prestriate cortex and then to posterior parietal cortex.

8. Prosopagnosia is:

    a. an inability to recognize faces.
    b. may be a general inability to recognize individual members of a class of visual stimuli.
    c. due to damage to striate cortex.
    d. due to damage to posterior parietal cortex.

9. Projections from the amygdala-pyriform area of the olfactory system:

    a. go to the thalamus and frontal cortex.
    b. go to the limbic system.
    c. convey information relevant to conscious perception of odors.
    d. convey information relevant to the emotional response to odors.

10. Selective attention is characterized by:

    a. the ability to restrict the flow of sensory information to your conscience.
    b. the ability to focus on all of the sensory stimuli that are present in your environment.
    c. unconscious monitoring of the environment for potentially relevant stimuli.
    d. increased blood flow to the secondary sensory cortex of the system under study.

B. Modified True-False and Fill-in-the Blank Section. If the statement is true, write TRUE in the blank provided. If the statement is false, write FALSE as well as the word or words that will make the statement true if they replaced the highlighted word or words in the original statement. If the statement is incomplete, write the word or words that will complete it.

1. True or False: **<u>Functional homogeneity</u>** characterizes the organization of sensory systems.

          A: _____

2. _____ are a product of the combined activity of the many cortical areas of each sensory system.

3. By definition, cortex that receives information from more than one sensory modality is called _____ cortex.

4. Cortically blind people can often provide information about visual stimuli (e.g., direction of movement) while claiming not to see anything; this phenomenon is called _____.

5. Many patients with extensive scotomas are unaware of them because of the phenomenon of _____.

6. True or False: A person who is unable to smell is suffering from an **agnosia.**

   A: _____

7. An agnosia for faces is called _____.

8. In terms of visual information, the posterior parietal cortex is part of the _____ pathway.

9. The ability to subconsciously monitor the contents of several simultaneous conversations while attending consciously to another is called the _____ phenomenon.

10. True or False: The **President** is attached to the oval window.

    A: _____

11. Auditory hair cells are located in the _____ membrane of the organ of Corti.

12. The auditory system is organized _____.

13. The medial and lateral _____ play a role in the localization of sounds in space.

14. True or False: The **interoceptive system** is responsible for the perception of the position of various parts of the body on the basis of input from receptors in muscles and joints.

    A: _____

15. The identification of stimuli by touch is called _____.

16. The largest most deeply positioned cutaneous receptor is the _____ corpuscle.

17. Perception of both cutaneous pain and temperature is mediated by receptors called _____.

18. The longest axons in the body ascend from the toes in the _____ of the spinal white matter.

19. True or False: Lesions to the **ventral posterior nucleus** of the thalamus reduced deep chronic pain without disrupting cutaneous sensitivity.

    A: _____

20. Somatosensory neurons carrying detailed information about touch ascend to the dorsal column nuclei, where they synapse on neurons whose axons decussate and ascend in the _____ to the ventral posterior nuclei .

20. The spinothalamic tract, the spinoreticular tract, and the spinotectal tract compose the _____ system.

21. SI is in the _____ gyrus of the parietal lobes.

22. SI comprises _____ independent parallel strips of cortical tissue.

23. The area of the body that is innervated by the left and right dorsal roots of a given segment of the spinal cord is called a _____.

24. _____ is the failure to recognize parts of one's own body.

25. Prefrontal _____ has been shown to reduce the emotional impact of pain, but it does not alter pain thresholds.

26. Neurons in the anterior portions of the auditory cortex respond specifically to _____-frequency sounds.

27. The discovery of opiate receptors in the brain suggested that the body might produce its own _____ opiates.

28. Patients lacking a sense of smell are said to be _____; those lacking a sense of taste are said to be _____.

29. Odoriferous chemicals released by an animal that influence the behavior of its conspecifics are called _____.

30. The axons of olfactory receptor cells enter the _____.

31. All tastes can be produced by combinations of four component tastes: sweet, _____, _____, and _____.

32. The _____ nucleus in the thalamus relays both somatosensory and gustatory information.

33. Single-unit recording studies suggest that selective attention is linked to activity in _____ cortex.

34. The interactions between primary sensory cortex, secondary sensory cortex, and association cortex are governed by three principles: 1) _____; 2) _____; and 3) _____.

35. A person who is unable to describe the size, location, shape, and movement of objects likely has damage to their _____.

C. Short Answer Section. In no more than 4 sentences, answer each of the following questions.

1. Describe the location and function of the four areas of the neocortex that are involved in vision.

2. Describe one possible path that auditory information could take from the ear to primary auditory cortex.

3. The chemical senses participate in some interesting forms of learning; what are they?

4. Describe the differences between Ungerleider and Mishkin's "where" model of what the dorsal stream of visual information does and Goodale and Milner's "how" model.

5. What is the functional significance of fast and slow receptor adaptation?

6. What is the cocktail-party phenomenon? What does it tell us about selective attention?

Mark your answers to the practice examination; the correct answers follow. On the basis of your performance, plan the final stages of your studying.

Chapter 8

Answers to the Practice Examination

A. Multiple Choice Section

1. a, b, c
2. b
3. b, c
4. a, c
5. b

6. a
7. a, d
8. a, b
9. a, b, c, d
10. a, c, d

B. Modified True/False and Fill-in-the-Blank Section

1. F; functional segregation
2. Perceptions
3. association
4. blindsight
5. completion
6. F; anosmia
7. prosopagnosia
8. dorsal stream
9. cocktail
10. F; stapes
11. basilar
12. tonotopically
13. superior olives
14. F; proprioceptive
15. stereognosis
16. Pacinian
17. free nerve endings
18. dorsal columns

19. F; intralaminar and parafascicular nuclei
20. medial lemnisci
21. postcentral
22. four
23. dermatome
24. Asomatognosia
25. lobotomy
26. high-frequency
27. endogenous
28. anosmic; ageusic
29. pheromones
30. olfactory bulbs
31. salty; bitter; sour
32. ventral posterior
33. secondary sensory
34. hierarchical organization; functional segregation; parallel processing
35. posterior parietal lobe.

C. Short Answer Section

1. Mention primary visual cortex (receives information from lateral geniculate nuclei of thalamus); prestriate cortex (secondary visual cortex; processes information from striate or primary visual cortex); posterior parietal cortex (the where/how system; the final region of the dorsal stream pathway); inferotemporal cortex (the what system; the final region of the ventral stream pathway).

2. Mention auditory nerve > ipsilateral cochlear nucleus > superior olives > lateral lemniscus > inferior colliculi > medial geniculate nuclei of thalamus > primary auditory cortex.

3. Mention conditioned taste aversions; conditioned taste preferences; odor-based feeding or copulatory preferences.

4. Mention that the "where" model suggests that dorsal and ventral streams process different types of information; "how" model suggests that information is the same but it is used in different ways by the two systems; mention support for "how" model.

5. Mention mixture of transient and continuous activity produces variety of sensations for a given stimulus; slow adapting receptors often convey information that is unconsciously processed; constant change in stimulus often helps in identification of objects by keeping fast adapting receptors activated.

Chapter 9

THE SENSORIMOTOR SYSTEM

I.   Jeopardy Study Items

With reference to Chapter 9 of BIOPSYCHOLOGY, write the correct answer to each of the following questions and the correct question for each of the following answers.

1. Describe the hierarchical organization of the sensorimotor system.

2. What is the effect on behavior of eliminating somatosensory feedback from the arms?

3.   A: ballistic movement

4.   A: posterior parietal cortex

5. Which sensory systems send information to the posterior parietal cortex?

6.   A: frontal eye fields

7. What is apraxia, and what lesions produce it?

8.   A: constructional apraxia

9. What is contralateral neglect, and what lesions produce it?

10. Describe the connectivity of the dorsolateral prefrontal cortex.

11.   A: memory fields

12.   A: supplementary motor area and premotor cortex

13. What evidence suggests that the supplementary motor area is involved in the planning of voluntary movements?

14.   A: it is in the precentral gyrus

15. What is the function of the supplementary motor area?

16. What is the function of the premotor cortex?

17. What is unusual about the receptive fields of bimodal cells in premotor cortex?

18.   A: precentral gyrus

19. What is the motor homunculus? What areas of the body are overrepresented?

20. What is stereognosis? What kind of sensory feedback underlies this ability?

21. What are the effects of damaging primary motor cortex?

22.   A: xenon 133

23. Describe the finger-maze task used by Roland and his colleagues; what were the results of this experiment?

24. What is the sensorimotor function of the cerebellum and basal ganglia?

25. What are the effects of cerebellar damage?

26.   A: they are part of a loop that receives input from the neocortex and transmits it back to the neocortex via the thalamus

27. What role are the basal ganglia thought to play in sensorimotor function?

28.   A: TANS

29. Describe the dorsolateral corticospinal tract.

30.   A: Betz cells

31. What is unique about the dorsolateral corticospinal tract projections to the digits in primates?

32. What are the differences between the dorsolateral corticospinal tract and the dorsolateral corticorubrospinal tract?

33.   A: "rubro"

34. Two motor pathways descend in the ventromedial portions of the spinal cord. What are the differences between them?

35.   A: the tectum, the vestibular nucleus, and the reticular formation

36. Compare and contrast the dorsolateral and ventromedial
    motor pathways.

37. What was the effect of transecting the left and right
    dorsolateral corticospinal tracts in monkeys?

38. What was the effect of transecting the dorsolateral
    corticorubrospinal tracts in monkeys whose dorsolateral
    corticospinal tracts had already been transected?

39.   A: this induced severe postural abnormalities

40. What is the difference between a motor unit and a motor
    pool?

41.   A: neuromuscular junction

42. What are the differences between fast muscle fibers and
    slow muscle fibers?

43.   A: flexors and extensors

44.   A: synergistic and antagonistic

45. What is the difference between dynamic contraction and
    isometric contraction?

46. What are the main structural and functional differences between Golgi tendon organs and muscle spindles?

47. What is the purpose of intrafusal muscle?

48.   A: patellar tendon reflex

49. What is the function of stretch reflexes?

50. How do muscle-spindle feedback circuits mediate the stretch reflex?

51. What evidence suggests that the withdrawal reflex is not monosynaptic?

52. What is reciprocal innervation?

53. What is cocontraction? What is its functional significance to movement?

54.   A: it is mediated by Renshaw cells

55. What evidence is there that the central motor programs for walking are in the spinal cord -- at least in cats?

56. How do we get our central sensorimotor programs?

57. Describe Fentress' research that suggested that some fundamental central motor control programs are inherited.

58.   A: response chunking and changing levels of control

59. What is a key principle of the chunking hypothesis of sensorimotor learning?

60. What are the two major advantages of shifting the level of control to lower levels of the sensorimotor system during sensorimotor learning?

Once you have completed the jeopardy study items, study them. Practice bidirectional studying; make sure that you know the correct answer to every question and the correct question for every answer.

II.   Essay Study Questions

Using Chapter 9 of BIOPSYCHOLOGY, write an outline of the answer to each of the following essay study questions.

1. Describe three general principles of sensorimotor function.

2. What three lines of evidence support the view that the posterior parietal cortex integrates the sensory information that is the basis for initiating voluntary responses?

3. Describe and interpret the cortical blood-flow studies of Roland and his colleagues.

4. Contrast the effects of cerebellar damage and primary motor cortex damage on motor behavior.

5. Describe the structure and function of the four descending motor pathways.

6. Describe and interpret the classic studies of Lawrence and Kuypers.

7. Draw the muscle-spindle feedback circuit, and by referring to it explain the neurophysiological basis of the stretch reflex.   What is the function of the stretch reflex?

8. Discuss the concept of central sensorimotor programs.

9. What two changes to central motor programs are thought to be the basis of sensorimotor learning?

10. Discuss the similarities between the organization and function of a big business and your sensorimotor system.

When you have answered the essay study questions, memorize your outlines to prepare for your upcoming examination.

III.   Practice Examination

After completing most of your studying of Chapter 9, but at least 24 hours before your formal examination, write the following practice examination.

A. Multiple-Choice Section. Circle the correct answer for each question; *REMEMBER that some questions may have more than one correct answer.*

1. Which lesions are commonly associated with contralateral neglect?

    a. bilateral frontal cortex lesions
    b. left temporal cortex lesions
    c. right posterior parietal cortex lesions
    d. bilateral supplementary motor area lesions

2. Which of the following areas of cortex is somatotopically organized?

    a. primary motor cortex
    b. supplementary motor cortex
    c. premotor cortex
    d. posterior parietal cortex

3. Renshaw cells mediate:

    a. cocontraction.
    b. mutual inhibition.
    c. lateral inhibition.
    d. recurrent collateral inhibition.

4. The advantage of cocontraction is that it:

    a. makes movements quicker.
    b. makes movements smoother.
    c. insulates us from the effects of unexpected external forces.
    d. shifts responsibility for a movement to other muscle groups.

5. Fentress (1973) showed that adult mice raised from birth without forelimbs:

    a. still made the patterns of shoulder movements typical of grooming in their species.
    b. made the tongue, head, and eye movements that would normally have occurred with specific shoulder movements in intact grooming mice.
    c. would often interrupt ostensible grooming sequences to lick a cage mate.
    d. "chunk" movements in a manner not observed in animals that have their forelimbs intact.

6. During sensorimotor learning, there is a transfer of control from higher to lower sensorimotor circuits. One major advantage of this transfer is that it:

    a. frees the higher levels of the nervous system to deal with more complex issues.
    b. increases the speed of movements.
    c. increases conscious awareness of the response.
    d. allows novel movements to be connected together.

7. In contrast to the descending ventromedial motor pathways, the dorsolateral motor pathways:

    a. control muscles capable of fine movements.
    b. controls one side of the body.
    c. is hierarchically organized.
    d. is chunked.

8. The primary motor cortex is:

    a. organized so that each area of the body is equally represented.
    b. organized somatopically.
    c. the point of convergence of cortical sensorimotor signals.
    d. located in the parietal lobe.

9. Each skeletal muscle is:

    a. comprised of hundreds of thousands of muscle fibers.
    b. a flexor.
    c. usually comprised of fast-twitch fibers.
    d. synergistic.

10. Antagonistic muscles are:

    a. comprised of flexors and extensors that oppose one another's action at a joint.
    b. innervated by the same group of neurons.
    c. reciprocally innervated, so that when one contracts the other relaxes.
    d. essential to smooth movements, with the nature of the movement dependent upon adjustment in the level of relative cocontraction.

B. Modified True-False and Fill-in-the Blank Section. If the statement is true, write TRUE in the blank provided. If the statement is false, write FALSE as well as the word or words that will make the statement true if they replaced the highlighted word or words in the original statement. If the statement is incomplete, write the word or words that will complete it.

1. Most movements are guided by sensory feedback; however, _____ are not.

2. Many adjustments in motor output that occur in response to sensory feedback are controlled by the _____ of the sensorimotor hierarchy.

3. Posterior parietal cortex is classified as _____ cortex because it receives sensory input from more than one sensory system.

4. True or False: Muscles that bend a joint are called **extensors.**

        A: _____

5. Although the symptoms of _____ are bilateral, it is often produced by unilateral damage to the left parietal lobe.

6. Patients with deficits on the block design subtest of the WAIS are said to suffer from _____.

7. True or False: The premotor cortex is considered to be **secondary motor cortex**.

    A: _____

8. According to the cortical blood-flow studies of Roland and his colleagues, the _____ provides sensory information to both the secondary motor areas and the _____ develops and executes programs for controlling the sequencing of motor output.

    A: _____

9. The ventromedial-cortico-brainstem-spinal tract interacts with several brainstem nuclei; these include the _____, which receives auditory and visual information about spatial location, and the _____, which receives information about balance from the semicircular canals of the inner ear.

10. A _____ reflex is one that is elicited by a sudden external stretching of the muscle.

11. True or False: The **cerebellum** is involved in the modification of existing motor programs on the basis of sensory input.

    A: _____

12. The _____ receives most of the output of areas of secondary motor cortex:

    A: _____

Which of the following statements is associated with the basal ganglia, and which is associated with the cerebellum?

13. It is 10% of the mass of the brain, but it contains more than 50% of its neurons.

    A: _____

14. Diffuse damage produces severe disturbances of balance, gait, articulation of speech, and the control of eye movements.

    A: _____

15. Diffuse damage eliminates the ability to adapt central motor programs to changing environmental conditions.

    A: _____

16. Diffuse damage eliminates the ability to precisely control the direction, force, velocity, and amplitude of individual movements.

    A: _____

17. Part of a loop that receives input from the neocortex and transmits it back to the neocortex via the thalamus.

    A: _____

There are four major motor tracts that descend from the primary motor cortex to the spinal cord. Write the name of the tract associated with each of the following.

18. red nucleus: _____ tract

19. Betz cells: _____ tract

20. Some axons in this tract synapse directly on motor neurons: _____ tract

21. The axons in this tract synapse on interneurons that in turn synapse on motor neurons that project to the muscles of the arms and legs: _____ tract

22. tectum, reticular formation, and vestibular nucleus: _____ tract

23. The axons of this tract descend ipsilaterally from the primary motor cortex directly into the ventromedial spinal white matter: _____ tract

24. The two dorsolateral motor tracts differ from the two ventromedial motor tracts in two major respects. What are they?

a.

b.

25. Two muscles whose contraction produces the same joint movement are said to be _____; two whose contraction produces opposite joint movements are said to be _____.

26. True or False: A contraction that decreases muscle length is said to be an **isometric contraction**.

A: _____

27. The receptors in tendons are called _____; those in muscles are called _____.

28. _____ are sensitive to muscle length; _____ are sensitive to muscle tension or pull.

29. True or False: Associated with each muscle spindle is a thread-like muscle called a **Golgi tendon organ.**

A: _____

30. According to the _____, practice combines individual response elements into long sequences of behavior.

C. Short Answer Section. In no more than 4 sentences, answer each of the following questions.

1. Describe the circuitry of the stretch reflex. What is the function of this reflex?

2. Theories of sensorimotor learning describe two kinds of changes to central motor programs. Describe each type of learning and its role in the acquisition and control of movements.

3. Describe anatomy and function of the basal ganglia.

4. Label the schematic diagram of a muscle-spindle feedback circuit provided below.

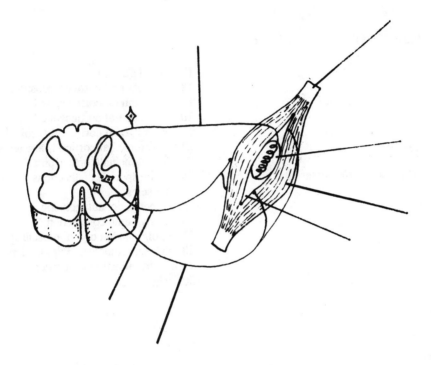

Mark your answers to the practice examination; the correct answers follow.   On the basis of your performance, plan the final stages of your studying.

Answers to Practice Examination

A. Multiple Choice Section

1. c
2. a, b, c
3. d
4. b, c
5. a, b, c

6. a, b
7. a, b
8. b, c
9. a
10. a, c, d

B. Modified True/False and Fill-in-the-Blank Section

1. ballistic movements
2. spinal circuits
3. association
4. F; flexors
5. apraxia
6. constructional apraxia
7. True
8. posterior parietal cortex; supplementary motor cortex
9. tectum; vestibular nucleus
10. stretch
11. True
12. primary motor cortex
13. cerebellum
14. cerebellum
15. cerebellum
16. basal ganglia

17. basal ganglia
18. dorsolateral corticorubrospinal
19. dorsolateral corticospinal
20. dorsolateral corticospinal
21. dorsolateral corticorubrospinal
22. ventromedial cortico-brainstem-spinal
23. ventromedial corticospinal
24. more specific connections; activate distal muscles
25. synergistic; antagonistic
26. F; dynamic contraction
27. Golgi tendon organ; muscle spindle
28. Muscle spindles; Golgi tendon organs
29. F; intrafusal muscle fiber
30. chunking hypothesis

C. Short Answer Section

1. Mention muscle spindles; stretch of the muscle (e.g., the patellar tendon reflex); stretch conveyed by spindle afferent neurons to dorsal horn; direct activation of motor neurons in ventral horn; contraction of stretched muscle; functions to keep external forces from altering the intended position of the body.

2. Mention chunking (programs for individual movements combined into novel, longer sequences); changing level of control of movement (from cortex to brainstem/spinal circuitry; frees cortex for other tasks and speeds movement).

3. Mention extensive reciprocal connectivity to motor cortex; lack of direct connections to motor neurons suggests modulatory role; involvement in sensorimotor learning.

4. See Figure 9.14 in BIOPSYCHOLOGY.

5. See Figure 9.4 in BIOPSYCHOLOGY.

Chapter 10

THE BIOPSYCHOLOGY OF EATING

I.   Jeopardy Study Items

With reference to Chapter 10 of BIOPSYCHOLOGY, write the correct answer to each of the following questions and the correct question for each of the following answers.

1.   A: digestion

2. What are the three forms of energy that the body receives
        as a consequence of digestion?

3. What are the three forms of energy that the body stores?

4. Why is it more efficient for the body to store energy in the
        form of fat?

5.   A: cephalic, absorptive, and fasting phases

6. Describe the role of insulin in the cephalic and fasting
        phases of energy metabolism.

7. Describe the role of glucagon in the fasting phase of
   energy metabolism.

8.   A: gluconeogenesis

9.   A: the set-point assumption

10. What three components are shared by all set-point
    systems?

11. What were the two set-point theories of hunger and
    feeding that evolved in the 1940s and 1950s?

12. From an evolutionary perspective, what is wrong with
    set-point theories of hunger and feeding?

13.   A: taste, learning, and social influences

14. What is the key idea behind the positive-incentive theory
    of feeding?

15. Why do most humans have a preference to sweet or fatty
    foods?

16. What is a conditioned taste aversion?

17. Why is it often difficult to consume a balanced diet in today's "fast-food" society?

18. What kinds of factors detemine the frequency with which a person will eat?

19. According to Woods, what is the cause of premeal hunger?

20.   A: satiety

21.   A: sham eating

22. What is nutritive density, and how does it alter feeding behavior?

23.   A: the appetizer effect

24. What effect does the number of flavors available at a meal have on feeding behavior?

25. Describe the phenomenon of sensory-specific satiety.

26. What are two consequences of sensory-specific satiety?

27. Why do blood glucose levels often drop just before a meal?

28. What are the effects in rats of large, bilateral lesions of the ventromedial region of the hypothalamus?

29.   A: static and dynamic phases

30. Why do VMH-lesioned rats sometimes seem less hungry than unlesioned control rats?

31. What are the effects in rats of large, bilateral lesions of the lateral region of the hypothalamus?

32. Why do VMH lesioned rats become obese?

33.   A: lipogenesis and lipolysis

34. Damage to which two structures can produce hyperphagia that is similar to that attributed to VMH lesions?

35. Although the LH is not a feeding center, what evidence suggests that it does contain neurons involved with the incentive properties of food?

36.   A: vagus nerve

37. What evidence indicates that signals from the stomach are not necessary for hunger or for body weight regulation?

38. How did Koopmans' "stomach transplant" study support the idea that the stomach has some role in satiety and feeding?

39.   A: cholecystokinin

40. Which CCK receptors seem to be important to the peptide's effect on feeding behavior?

41.   A: adiposity

42. What evidence suggests that levels of insulin in the CNS is important to the regulation of feeding behavior.

43. Describe the beneficial effects of dietary restriction.

44.   A: diet-induced thermogenesis

45. What is the difference between a set-point and a settling-point?

46. Describe the leaky-barrel model of settling-point theory.

47.   A: isotonic solutions

48.   A: interstitial fluid, blood, and cerebrospinal fluid

49. What regulates the body's water and sodium balance?

50. How does the body react to a decrease in the body's water
     resources?

51.   A: hypovolemia and cellular dehydration

52. Why do salty foods make you thristy?

53. How is cellular dehydration induced in experimental
    subjects so that its effects can be studied independently of
    the other effects of water deficits?

54.   A: osmoreceptors

55.   A: lateral preoptic area of the hypothalamus

56. How do osmoreceptors induce thirst?

57. How is hypovolemia induced in experimental animals so
    that its effects can be studied independently of the other
    effects of water deficits?

58.   A: baroreceptors and blood flow receptors

59.   A: nephrectomized

60. What is the relation between renin, angiotensin II, and
    aldosterone?

61.   A: dipsogen

62. What suggested that the subfornical organ might play a
    role in angiotensin-II's dipsogenic effect?

63. Which transmitter is involved in the role of the
    subfornical organ in drinking behavior in the rat?

64. What suggests that drinking in response to naturally
    occurring water deficits is primarily the result of cellular
    dehydration?

65.   A: it is spontaneous drinking

66. Why is the termination of drinking behavior difficult to
    account for using set-point models?

67.   A: saccharin elation effect

68.   What is schedule-induced polydipsia?

69.   Why have evolutionary factors contributed to the
      problem of obesity?

70.   What two individual differences play a role in obesity?

71.   What are the symptoms of anorexia nervosa and bulimia
      nervosa?

72.   In what way are the attitidues of many anorectics about
      food somewhat paradoxical?

Once you have completed the jeopardy study items, study them. Practice bidirectional studying; make sure that you know the correct answer to every question and the correct question for every answer.

II.   Essay Study Questions

Using Chapter 10 of BIOPSYCHOLOGY, write an outline of the answer to each of the following essay study questions.

1.   Describe that various factors that influence spontaneous drinking.

2.   Summarize the hypothalamic set-point model of the physiology of eating, which was dominant in the 1950s and 1960s. On what findings was the model based?

3.   Describe and critically evaluate the idea that increases and decreases from an internal set point (for blood glucose or for body fat) are critical factors in satiety and hunger, respectively.

4. What evidence suggests that there is a gastrointestinal peptide satiety signal?

5. How has the view of the role of the hypothalamus in eating changed since the 1950s? Specifically, how have the hyperphagia and obesity produced by large bilateral VMH lesions and the cessation of feeding produced by LH lesions been reinterpreted?

6. Describe some of the factors that influence when we eat and how much we eat.

7. The idea that eating is a response to energy deficits has been replaced by postive-incentive theories of feeding. Describe this theory and explain why is has replaced the idea of feeding as a response to energy deficits.

8.   What is the settling-point (leaky-barrel) model of the regulation of ingestive behaviors? Contrast it with the set-point (thermostat) model.

9.   Describe the evidence that supports the idea that the lateral preoptic area and the subfornical organ play key roles in the regulation of drinking behavior.

10. Describe the compensatory events that are triggered by a decrease in blood pressure and blood flow.

11. Most of the drinking that we do is spontaneous drinking, yet most the research on the physiology of drinking has focused on drinking induced by cellular dehydration or hypovolemia. Discuss.

12. Describe the symptoms and prognosis of anorexia nervosa.

13. Describe the three phases of energy metabolism and their control by the pancreatic hormones insulin and glucagon.

14. Discuss the neural bases for drinking behavior induced by hypovolemia and cellular dehydration, respectively.

15. "Obesity is the product of evolution gone awry". Discuss this statement and its implications for how obesity is viewed and treated.

When you have answered the essay study questions, memorize your outlines to prepare for your upcoming examination.

III. Practice Examination

After completing most of your studying of Chapter 10, but at least 24 hours before your formal examination, write the following practice examination.

A. Multiple-Choice Section. Circle the correct answer for each question; *REMEMBER that some questions may have more than one correct answer.*

1. In rats, bilateral LH lesions produce:

   a. aphagia.
   b. adipsia.
   c. apraxia.
   d. agnosia.

2. Insulin and glucagon are synthesized and released by the:

   a. liver.
   b. duodenum.
   c. pancreas.
   d. kidney.

3. During the fasting phase, the body (excluding the brain) obtains most of its energy from:

   a. glucose.
   b. free fatty acids.
   c. ketones.
   d. glycogen

4. The research of Woods and Porte suggests that the effects of the level of body fat on eating are mediated by changes in the level of:

   a. insulin in the cerebrospinal fluid.
   b. glucose in the cerebrospinal fluid.
   c. lipids in the blood.
   d. lipids in the cerebrospinal fluid.

5. Koopmans implanted an extra stomach into rats. He found:

   a. evidence that a gastric satiety factor was being released from the implant into the blood.
   b. that injections of food into the implanted stomach reduced food consumption.
   c. that neural signals play an important role in eating.
   d. that infusion of glucose into the bloodstream increased the contractions in both stomachs.

6. Bilateral VMH lesions increase:

   a. lipogenesis.
   b. lipolysis.
   c. eating.
   d. drinking

Chapter 10

7. The evidence suggests that the hyperphagia produced by large bilateral VMH lesions is:

    a. unrelated to the weight gain.
    b. to a large degree a secondary consequence of an increase in lipogenesis.
    c. to a large degree a secondary consequence of an increase in lipolysis.
    d. caused by hypoinsulemia.

8. In the first part of an important experiment by Weingarten, a buzzer-and-light conditional stimulus was presented before each meal. In the second part of this experiment:

    a. the conditional stimulus was shown to decrease eating.
    b. the conditional stimulus caused the rats to start eating, even if they had just finished eating a meal.
    c. feeding behavior was found to be extinguished.
    d. the conditional stimulus had become an extinguished stimulus.

9. Which of the following is the basis for a mammal's ability to select a healthy combination of foods in its natural environment?

    a. a preference for sweet tastes
    b. a preference for salty tastes
    c. a mechanism that increases salt preference when there is a sodium deficiency
    d. the ability for the good and bad effects that might follow the consumption of a food to influence the incentive value of its taste

10. The peptide CCK may reduce feeding behavior by:

    a. increasing the absorption of food from the duodenum.
    b. altering the release of insulin from the hypothalamus.
    c. altering neural activity in the CNS.
    d. slowing the release of food from the stomach.

11. Osmotic pressure draws:

    a. water from hypertonic solutions.
    b. water from hypotonic solutions.
    c. solutes from hypertonic solutions.
    d. solutes from hypotonic solutions.

12. The fact that small does of a hypertonic solution injected into a carotid artery can elicit drinking suggests that there are:

    a. blood-flow receptors in the brain.
    b. blood-pressure receptors in the brain.
    c. osmoreceptors in the brain.
    d. blood-pressure receptors in the carotid artery.

13. Nicolaidis and Roland (1975) added quinine to the drinking water of rats. This:

    a. increased the amount that the rats drank.
    b. decreased the amount that the rats drank.
    c. increased the body weight of the rats.
    d. led to several deaths from dehydration.

14. Which of the following is often a symptom of anorexia nervosa?

    a. weight loss
    b. hyperphagia
    c. unrealistic body image
    d. increased pleasure from food

15. People who are not anorectic but who display recurring cycles of binging, purging, and fasting are said to suffer from:

    a. hyperphagia.
    b. anorexia nervosa.
    c. hypophagia.
    d. bulimia nervosa.

16. People who suffer from obesity:

    a. will lose weight on a long-term basis only if they adopt permanent lifestyle changes.
    b. have an imbalance between energy intake and energy expenditures.
    c. can lose significant amounts of weight by doing nothing more than exercising.
    d. have no control over their behavior.

17. Sensory-specific satiety is an important factor in gustatory behavior because it:

    a. ensures that we do not eat too much.
    b. encourages animals to eat different types of food and thus consume a balanced diet.
    c. encourages animals to eat a lot in times of food abundance.
    d. maintains our interest in food.

18. Animals with lesions of the LH may cease eating because of:

    a. unintended damage to areas such as the dorsal noradrenergic bundle.
    b. increased blood insulin levels and the resulting lipogenesis.
    c. generalized deficits in motor and sensory function.
    d. cells that respond to the incentive properties of food.

19. Canon and Washburn's report that hunger is due to stomach contractions was:

    a. based on Washburn's introspections and his ability to swallow a balloon.
    b. disproved when it was shown that surgical removal of the stomach did not eliminate hunger pangs.
    c. supported by Koopman's "stomach transplant" studies.
    d. disproven by the effect that CCK has on feeding behavior.

20. Drinking behavior:

    a. is less important than feeding behavior to short-term survival.
    b. that is produced by naturally occurring deficits is most likely a response to cellular dehydration
    c. is not generally affected by factors such as flavor or food.
    d. normally occurs in the absence of any deficit.

21. Feeding and drinking behaviors can both be affected by:

    a. lesions of the LH.
    b. learning.
    c. flavor.
    d. alterations in their set points.

22. The subfornical organ:

    a. plays a key role in gustatory behaviors.
    b. plays a key role in drinking behavior elicited by bloodborne angiotensin II.
    c. plays a key role in drinking behavior elicited by centrally released angiotensin II.
    d. releases the transmitter acetylcholine to mediate its effects on drinking behavior.

23. Injections of norepinephrine, GABA, or neuropeptide Y into the paraventricular nucleus of the hypothalamus elicits:

    a. a significant increase in all gustatory behavior.
    b. a significant decrease in all gustatory behavior.
    c. a significant increase in the ingestion of carbohydrates.
    d. a significant increase in the ingestion of fats.

24. Animals who have their food intake restricted to levels 30%-60% of free-feeding control animals:

    a. are sleeker and livelier.
    b. are likely to develop adipsia.
    c. live longer, healthier lives.
    d. live shorter though healthier lives.

25. Decreasing a person's food intake:

    a. will decrease the efficiency with which they utilize the food that they do consume.
    b. is a good way to reduce their body weight.
    c. will increse the efficiency with which they utilize the food that they do consume.
    d. will reset their body fat set point.

B. Modified True-False and Fill-in-the Blank Section. If the statement is true, write TRUE in the blank provided. If the statement is false, write FALSE as well as the word or words that will make the statement true if they replaced the highlighted word or words in the original statement. If the statement is incomplete, write the word or words that will complete it.

1. The _____ phase of feeding may begin with the smell, sight, or simple thought of food.

2. True or False: **Glucagon** may play a role in the regulation of feeding via receptors in the hypothalamus.

    A: _____

3. Drinking in the absence of deficits is called _____.

4. The calories contained in a given volume of food reflects the _____ of that food.

5. The early theory that the signals from the _____ play a critical role in hunger and satiety was abandoned when it was noted that surgical removal of this organ did not eliminate hunger pangs.

6. In a _____ feeding experiment, food that is eaten never reaches the stomach because it passes out of the body through an tube implanted in the eosophagus.

7. Many studies of feeding have been based on the premise that eating is controlled by a system designed to maintain the homeostasis of the body's energy resources by responding to deviations from a hypothetical _____.

8. The body has three sources of energy: glucose, _____, and _____.

9. Excessive drinking caused by the presentation of food on an intermittent basis is called _____.

10. True or False: Sensory-specific satiety helps to **restrict** the variety of foods that an animals will eat.

    A: _____

11. The point made by the saccharin elation effect is that drinking a beverage temporarily _____ the incentive value of similar-tasting beverages.

12. Presenting a rat with a different-tasting palatable solution every 15 minutes will induce _____ in most subjects.

13. _____ causes the kidney to absorb much of the sodium that would otherwise have been lost in the urine.

14. According to the pre-eminent theory of the 1950s and 60s, the _____ nucleus of the hypothalamus is a hunger center, and the _____ nucleus is a satiety center.

15. The syndrome produced by bilateral VMH lesions in rats has two phases: the _____ phase is first and the _____ phase is second.

16. The role played by taste in the development of satiety is illustrated by the phenomenon of _____ satiety, in which eating a food may produce satiety for the taste of that food while having little effect on the incentive properties of other tastes.

17. There are three stages of metabolism associated with a meal; in chronological order, these are:

    a. the _____ phase

    b. the _____ phase

    c. the _____ phase

18. Osmoreceptors appear to be located in the _____ nucleus of the hypothalamus.

19. Insulin is released during the cephalic and _____ phases of metabolism, and glucagon is released during the _____ phase.

20. During starvation, the brain receives its energy from the glucose that is created by
_____ and from _____, which are breakdown products of body fat.

21. As an individual gains weight, there is often an increase in his or her body temperature that counteracts further weight gain by wasting calories. Such an increase in body temperature is commonly referred to as _____ thermogenesis.

22. Bombesin, glucagon, somatostatin, and _____ are peptide hormones that are released by the gastrointestinal tract and have been shown to reduce food intake.

23. Evidence suggests that the hyperphagia that is produced by large bilateral lesions to the VMH is caused in part by damage to the _____ nuclei of the hypothalamus or their connections.

24. In _____ drinking experiments, the water that a subject drinks flows down its esophagus and out of its body before it can be absorbed.

25. Two-thirds of the body's water is located _____.

26. True or False: Animals that are deficient in **a vitamin or mineral** have to learn which foods contain the vitamin or mineral.

    A: _____

27. Insulin may regulate feeding behavior by providing the brain with information about _____.

28. Osmoreceptors respond to cellular dehydration by increasing both drinking and the release of _____ hormone.

29. _____ are glue-like substances with molecules much too large to pass through cell membranes.

30. Both ADH and the activity of blood-flow receptors in the kidneys cause the kidneys to release _____, and this causes the formation of the peptide dipsogen, _____.

31. True or False: The release of **glucagon** causes the kidneys to reabsorb more sodium.

    A: _____

32. Cerebral angiotensin II receptors are located in the _____.

33. Angiotensin II produces an increase in blood pressure by constricting peripheral blood vessels and by triggering the release of _____ from the adrenal cortex.

34. True or False: High **cholecystokinin** levels stimulate the formation of ketones from free fatty acids.

    A: _____

35. Fat is the most efficient form of energy storage because a gram of fat holds _____ as many calories as a gram of glycogen, and fat does not absorb _____.

C. Short Answer Section. In no more than 4 sentences, answer each of the following questions.

1. Briefly describe how differences in enery intake and expenditure could conspire to produce a state of obesity.

2. Point out the flaws with the statement "You drink when you feel thirsty".

3. Describe the effects of LH lesions on ingestive behaviors.

4. How do osmoreceptors induce drinking behavior?

5. Many college students who live in dormitories find that they gain weight; given what you know about gustatory behavior, why should this be so?

6. What four pieces of evidence suggest that VMH lesions elicit feeding by increasing the storage of glucose as fat?

Mark your answers to the practice examination; the correct answers follow. On the basis of your performance, plan the final stages of your studying.

Answers to Practice Examination

A. Multiple Choice Section

1. a, b	10. c, d	19. a, b
2. c	11. b	20. b, d
3. b, c	12. c	21. a, b, c
4. a	13. b	22. b, d
5. a, b	14. a, c	23. c
6. a, c	15. d	24. a, c
7. b	16. a, b	25. c
8. b	17. b, c	
9. a, b, c, d	18. c	

B. Modified True/False and Fill-in-the-Blank Section

1. cephalic	19. absorptive; fasting
2. False; insulin	20. free fatty acids; ketones
3. spontaneous drinking	21. diet-induced thermogenesis
4. nutritive density	22. cholecyctokinin
5. stomach	23. paraventricular nucleus
6. sham	24. sham
7. set point	25. intracellularly
8. lipids; amino acids	26. True
9. schedule-induced polydipsia	27. adiposity
10. False; increase	28. ADH
11. reduces	29. Colloids
12. polydipsia	30. renin; angiotensin II
13. aldosterone	31. aldosterone
14. LH; VMH	32. subfornical organ
15. dynamic; static	33. aldosterone
16. sensory-specific satiety	34. False; glucagon
17. cephalic; absorptive; fasting	35. twice; water
18. lateral preoptic area	

C. Short Answer Section

1. Mention that hyperinsulinemia or exaggerated cephalic-phase insulin release can produce excessive lipogenesis; metabolic efficiency can differ greatly between individuals, resulting in differential weight gain with identical diets.

2. Mention that most drinking is spontaneous; it is greatly affected by flavor, the presence of food, and learning; animals usually drink in excess of their needs.

3. Mention that it produces aphagia (possibly as a result of impaired sensory and motor function) and adipsia (because the LH seems to have a role in the initiation of drinking behavior).

4. Mention direct activation of neural circuits and indirect activation through the release of ADH.

5. Mention factors that encourage excessive eating: cafeteria-style diet; scheduled meals; eating with other people.

6. Mention hyperinsulinemia; that VMH lesioned rats store more fat than unlesioned controls eating the same amount of food; that VMH lesions increase the use of energy derived from gluconeogenesis; that cutting the vagus nerve eliminates both the obesity and hyperphagia produced by VMH lesions.

Chapter 11

HORMONES AND SEX

I.   Jeopardy Study Items

With reference to Chapter 11 of BIOPSYCHOLOGY, write the correct answer to each of the following questions and the correct question for each of the following answers.

1. What is the "mamawawa"?

2.   A: exocrine glands and endocrine glands

3. What is copulation?

4.   A: testes and ovaries

5.   A: XX and XY

6. Androgens, estrogens, and progestins are the three main classes of gonadal hormones; which is the most noteworthy hormone in each class?

7.   A: gonadotropins

8. The pituitary comprises two independent endocrine glands; what are they?

9. What is the major difference between the pattern of gonadal and gonadotropic hormone release in males and females?

10.   A: vasopressin and oxytocin

11.   A: by the paraventricular and supraoptic nuclei

12. What is the hypothalamopituitary portal system?

13. How was thyrotropin- releasing hormone first isolated?

14. What is the difference between a releasing factor and a releasing hormone?

15.   A: FSH and LH

16. What roles do negative feedback and positive feedback
     play in the neuroendocrine system?

17. What is ovulation?

18.   A: pulsatile hormone release

19. How does H-Y antigen control the differentiation of the
     primordial gonads?

20. How do androgens and Müllerian-inhibiting substance
     control the differentiation of the internal reproductive
     ducts?

21.   A: seminal vesicles and vas deferens

22.   A: the uterus and the fallopian tubes

23. What are the differences among castration, gonadectomy,
     orchidectomy, and ovariectomy?

24. What controls the development of male and female external reproductive organs?

25.

A: they are the female structures that develop from the same tissue as the head of the penis, the shaft of the penis, and the scrotum in the male

26. Why are rats convenient subjects for studying the effects of hormones on brain development?

27. What did early gonadal transplantation research suggest about sexual differentiation?

28. What is the aromatization hypothesis?

29. What evidence supports the hypothesis that aromatization plays a critical role in the sexual differentiation of the rat brain?

30.

A: alpha fetoprotein

31.

A: mounting, intromission, and ejaculation

32. What is lordosis?

33.   A: secondary sex characteristics

34. The levels of which hormones increase during puberty?

35.   A: androstenedione

36. What are the symptoms of androgenic insensitivity in genetic males?

37. What hormonal factors cause androgenic insensitive genetic males to develop female bodies?

38.   A: it is caused by a deficiency in the release of cortisol, which results in the release of high levels of adrenal androgens

39. What happens to genetic adrenogenital females at puberty if they are not treated?

40. How was the sex of Money's famous ablatio-penis twin changed?

41.   A: the most puzzling aspect of its effects is the variability in the rate at which male sexual behavior declines

42. What are the effects of orchidectomy in adult males?

43. What are the effects of testosterone replacement injections in adult males?

44.   A: these findings suggest that androgens are responsible for maintaining sex drive in human females

45. What effect does ovariectomy have on women?

46. What are the effects of high doses of anabolic steroids in men and women?

47.   A: the sexually dimorphic nuclei

48. Which hormone influences the development of the sexually dimorphic nuclei?

49.   A: they approach and investigate receptive females, but they cannot successfully mount them

50. Which area of the hypothalamus is critical for the sexual
behavior of female rats?

51.   A: it facilitates lordosis

52. What evidence is there that sexual preference has a
genetic basis?

53.   A: they have been shown to influence sexual preference
in many species

54.   A: INAH 3

55. What were the results of LeVay's (1991) study of brain
structure and male homosexuality?

**Once you have completed the jeopardy study items, study them. Practice bidirectional studying; make sure
that you know the correct answer to every question and the correct question for every answer.**

II.   Essay Study Questions

Using Chapter 11 of BIOPSYCHOLOGY, write an outline to answer to each of the following essay study questions.

1. Describe how the posterior pituitary is controlled by the hypothalamus.

2. Describe how the anterior pituitary is controlled by the hypothalamus.

3. Summarize the factors that control the differentiation of the gonads, the internal reproductive ducts, and the external reproductive organs.

4. We are all genetically programmed to develop female bodies; genetic males develop male bodies only if their fundamentally female program of development is overruled by gonadal hormones. Explain and discuss.

5. How is the differentiation of the brain controlled by gonadal hormones? What is the aromatization hypothesis? What evidence suggests that aromatization is critical for the normal development of the male rat brain?

6. What are the effects of perinatal injection of testosterone on subsequent copulatory behavior in the adult female? What are the effects of a lack of early exposure to testosterone on subsequent copulatory behavior in the adult male?

7. What effects do hormones have on the development of secondary sex characteristics?

8. Describe the androgenic insensitivity syndrome. What does it indicate about the role of androgens in sexual development?

9. What is the adrenogenital syndrome? How is it treated? What are the consequences of nontreatment?

10. Describe the famous case of the identical twin suffering from ablatio penis. What does it suggest about the role of social factors in sexual development? What does it suggest about science?

11. What are the effects of orchidectomy and/or testosterone injections on adult human males? What are the effects of anabolic steroids on adult human males?

12. What are the effects of ovariectomy, adrenalectomy, estrogen injections, testosterone injections, and anabolic steroids on adult human females?

13. Describe the role of the hypothalamus in male and female sexual behavior.

14. Describe recent research on the relation between hypothalamic structure, gender, and sexual preference.

15. Describe the differences between amino-acid derivative hormones, peptide hormones, and steroid hormones.

When you have answered the essay study questions, memorize your outlines to prepare for your upcoming examination.

III.   Practice Examination

> *After completing most of your studying of Chapter 11, but at least 24 hours before your formal examination, write the following practice examination.*

A. Multiple-Choice Section. Circle the correct answer for each question; *REMEMBER that some questions may have more than one correct answer.*

1. The two types of glands in the body are the:

   a. exocrine glands
   b. pituitary glands
   c. adrenal glands
   d. endocrine glands

2. Every cell in the normal human body, with the exception of some sperm cells, have:

   a. 23 chromosomes.
   b. at least one Y chromosome.
   c. at least one X chromosome.
   d. a pair of X chromosomes.

3. Tropic hormones:

   a. are released from the anterior pituitary
   b. influence the release of hormones from other glands
   c. are released into the circulatory system
   d. regulate gonadal hormone release

4. Gonadotropin-releasing hormone directly stimulates the release of:

   a. estrogen.
   b. lutenizing hormone.
   c. follicle stimulating hormone.
   d. both b and c

5. Feedback in the neuroendocrine system is:

   a. usually negative.
   b. usually positive.
   c. always negative.
   d. always positive.

6. Behaviors by which females "solicit" males are called:

    a. naughty.
    b. lordotic.
    c. proceptive.
    d. receptive.

7. Orchidectomizing male rats shortly after birth:

    a. masculinizes their adult copulatory behavior.
    b. feminizes their adult copulatory behavior.
    c. demasculinizes their adult copulatory behavior.
    d. both b and c

8. Which sex chromosomes are possessed by somebody suffering from androgenic insensitivity syndrome?

    a. XY
    b. XX
    c. YY
    d. X

9. Which of the following is responsible for the pubertal feminization of androgen-insensitive males?

    a. androgens
    b. estrogens
    c. androstenedione
    d. progesterone

10. The subject of John Money's famous case study of ablatio penis was treated by

    a. castrating him.
    b. giving him estrogen injections at puberty.
    c. raising him as a girl.
    d. creating an artificial vagina.

11. Orchidectomy produces a decline in the interest in reproductive behavior and in the ability to engage in it. However:

    a. the rate of the decline varies markedly from woman to woman.
    b. the rate of the decline varies markedly from man to man.
    c. this decline is rarely complete in less than a year.
    d. both a and c

12. Although orchidectomy eventually eliminates reproductive behavior in virtually all cases, there is

    a. strong evidence of a correlation between sex drive and testosterone levels in healthy males.
    b. no strong evidence of a correlation between sex drive and testosterone levels in healthy males.
    c. no evidence that replacement injections can bring it back.
    d. both a and c

13. Which of the following statements about estradiol and female sexual behavior is/are NOT TRUE?

    a. estradiol makes cells in the hypothalamus insensitive to progesterone
    b. estradiol increases the number of progesterone receptors in the VMN of the hypothalamus
    c. estradiol enters cells in the VMN of the hypothalamus and influences gene expression
    d. injections of estradiol in the VMN of the hypothalamus induce estrus in ovariectomized female rats

14. Many male homosexuals are likely to become bisexual following:

    a. castration.
    b. injections of testosterone.
    c. injections of estrogen.
    d. none of the above

15. Evidence that differences in sexual orientation have a genetic basis include the observation(s) that

    a. the concordance rate for male homosexuality in monozygotic twin brothers is 52%.
    b. the concordance rate for male homosexuality in dizygotic twin brother is 22%.
    c. a gene exists on the X chromosome that plays a role in the development of sexual orientation.
    d. all of the above

B. Modified True-False and Fill-in-the Blank Section. If the statement is true, write TRUE in the blank provided. If the statement is false, write FALSE as well as the word or words that will make the statement true if they replaced the highlighted word or words in the original statement. If the statement is incomplete, write the word or words that will complete it.

1. True or False: Hormones influence sex by influencing the development from conception to sexual maturity of the **intellectual**, physiological, and behavioral characteristics that distinguish one as female or male.

        A: _____

2. A sperm and an ovum combine to form a _____.

3. Name the three major classes of gonadal hormones, and give one example of each.

    a._____; e.g., _____

    b._____; e.g., _____

    c._____; e.g., _____

4. The following sex steroids are released by the testes but not by the ovaries and adrenal cortex: _____.

5. The sex hormones released by the anterior pituitary are referred to as _____.

6. The pituitary dangles from the _____ on the end of the pituitary stalk.

7. The two hormones released by the posterior pituitary are _____.

8. The two hypothalamic nuclei that contain the cell bodies of the neurons that manufacture the hormones of the posterior pituitary are the _____ nuclei and the _____ nuclei.

9. True or False: Any vein that connects one capillary network with another is called a **portal** vein.

    A: _____

10. The only line of communication between the hypothalamus and the anterior pituitary is the _____ system.

11. The first releasing hormone to be isolated was _____ hormone.

12. Virtually all hormones are released from endocrine glands in _____.

13. _____ causes the medulla of each primordial gonad to develop into a testis.

14. At 6 weeks, each human fetus has two sets of reproductive ducts: a female _____ system and a male _____ system.

15. _____ substance causes the Müllerian system to degenerate and the testes to descend into the scrotum.

16. Female reproductive ducts develop as a result of _____.

17. True or False: Gonadectomy is the same thing as **orchidectomy**.

    A: _____

18. During development of the external reproductive organs the labioscrotal swellings grow into the _____ in males and the labia majora in females.

19. True or False: A neonatal female rat was ovariectomized. As an adult, its pattern of gonadotropin release was **cyclic**.

    A: _____

20. The _____ nuclei of the preoptic area are larger in male rats and humans than in female rats and humans.

21. All gonadal and adrenal sex hormones are _____ compounds.

22. It has been hypothesized that the conversion of testosterone to _____ is critical for testosterone to masculinize the brain.

23. True or False: In support of the aromatization hypothesis is the finding that **dihydrotestosterone** has no masculinizing effect on the rat brain.

    A: _____

24. The androgen, _____ stimulates the growth of pubic and axillary hair in pubertal females.

25. Many female babies suffering from _____ syndrome are born with an enlarged clitoris and partially fused labia.

26. The key hormones in maintaining the sex drive of human females are thought to be _____.

The following are side effects of anabolic steroid abuse. Which are more of a problem for males, and which are more of a problem for females?

    27.   hirsutism: females ___   males ___

    28.   gynecomastia: females ___   males ___

    29.   amenorrhea: females ___   males ___

30. True or False: The areas of the hypothalamus that are involved in male and female sexual behavior are the **medial preoptic area and ventromedial hypothalamus**, respectively.

        A: _____

C. Short Answer Section. In no more than 4 sentences, answer each of the following questions.

1. List the three major categories of hormones. Describe the <u>synthesis</u> of hormones in each major category.

2. How does the differentiation of the external reproductive organs differ from the differentiation of the gonads and the internal reproductive ducts?

3. Phoenix and colleagues (1959) were among the first to examine the effect of perinatal injection of testosterone on a genetic female's adult copulatory behavior. Describe the methods and results of the experiment.

4. What is the treatment for adrenogenital syndrome? What are the problems facing an individual suffering from an untreated case of adrenogenital syndrome?

5. Describe the effects of adult orchidectomy.

6. With respect to the hormonal control of reproductive behavior, women differ from the females of other mammalian species. How?

Mark your answers to the practice examination; the correct answers follow. On the basis of your performance, plan the final stages of your studying.

Answers to Practice Examination

A. Multiple Choice Section

1. a; d
2. c
3. a; b; c; d
4. d
5. a
6. c
7. d
8. a

9. b
10. a; b; c; d
11. b
12. b
13. a
14. d
15. d

B. Modified True/False and Fill-in-the-Blank Section

1. False; anatomical
2. zygote
3. a. androgens; testosterone
   b. estrogens; estradiol
   c. progestins; progesterone
4. none
5. gonadotropins
6. hypothalamus
7. vasopressin and oxytocin
8. paraventricular and supraoptic
9. True
10. hypothalamopituitary portal
11. thyrotropin-releasing
12. pulses
13. H-Y antigen
14. Müllerian; Wolffian
15. Müllerian inhibiting

16. a lack of testosterone during the critical period of fetal development
17. False; castration
18. scrotum
19. True
20. sexually dimorphic
21. steroid
22. estradiol
23. True
24. androstenedione
25. adrenogenital
26. androgens
27. females
28. males
29. females
30. True

C. Short Answer Section

1. Mention the (1) amino acid derivative hormones synthesized from an amino acid molecule (e.g., epinephrine), (2) peptide and protein hormones comprised of chains of amino acids, and (3) steroid hormones synthesized from cholesterol (e.g., androgens and estrogens).

2. In the case of external reproductive organs mention bipotentiality and the role of testosterone; in the case of the gonads and internal ducts mention Mηllerian system, Wolffian system, H-Y antigen, testosterone, and Mηllerian-inhibiting substance.

3. Mention that the researchers injected pregnant guinea pigs with testosterone, ovariectomized the resulting female offspring; at maturity, these offspring exhibited more male-like mounting behavior following an injection of testosterone and less lordosis following an injection of progesterone and estradiol.

4. Mention surgical correction of external genitals and cortisol administration; there is no way of knowing whether the adrenogenital female will be feminized or masculinized at puberty.

5. Mention reduced body hair, fat on the hips and chest, softening of the skin, reduced strength, impotence, sterility.

6. Their reproductive behavior is not under the control of gonadal hormones; ovariectomy and hormone replacement injections have no effect on it.

7. See Figure 11.5 in BIOPSYCHOLOGY.

Chapter 12

SLEEPING, DREAMING, AND CIRCADIAN RHYTHMS

I.   Jeopardy Study Items

With reference to Chapter 12 of BIOPSYCHOLOGY, write the correct answer to each of the following questions and the correct question for each of the following answers.

1. What does the case of Miss M. suggest?

2.   A: REMs or rapid eye movements

3.   A: the EEG, the EMG, and the EOG

4. What is the first-night phenomenon?

5.   A: alpha waves

6.   A: K complexes and sleep spindles

7. What are the largest and slowest of the normal EEG waves
   called?

8.   A: predominance of delta waves

9.   A: initial stage 1 and emergent stage 1

10.   A: paradoxical sleep

11. What term refers to both stage 3 and stage 4 sleep?

12. Sleep is commonly divided into two major categories.
    What are these two categories?

13. What are the physiological correlates of human REM
    sleep?

14. What is the strongest evidence that REM sleep is when
    people dream?

15.   A: somnambulism

16   A: despite what most people believe, they usually occur
                                         during stage 4 sleep; not during dreaming

17.   A: activation-synthesis hypothesis

18 What are lucid dreams?

19. What are the recuperative and circadian theories of sleep?

20.   A circadian rhythms

21.   A: free-running rhythms and free-running period

22. What are three important fundamental properties of free-
     running periods?

23. What is the evidence that animals can display free-
     running circadian rhythms without ever experiencing
     circadian zeitgebers?

24. What does the negative correlation between the duration
     of a person's sleep and the duration of the preceding
     period of wakefulness suggest?

25.   A: internal desynchronization

26.   A: phase advances and phase delays, respectively

27. What can be done to reduce the disruptive effects of shift work and jet lag?

28. What symptoms are experienced by a person who does not sleep for 5 days?

29.   A: surprisingly, they get only a few extra hours on the first night and perhaps the second

30. What sorts of activities are most disrupted by sleep deprivation?

31.   A: microsleeps

32. What is the carousel apparatus, and how is it used?

33. What are the two major effects of REM-sleep deprivation?

34.   A: although they block REM sleep, patients taking regular large doses display no obvious side effects

35. What five observations support the view that sleep's recuperative function is served specifically by stage 3 and stage 4 sleep?

36.   A: between the inferior and the superior colliculi

37.   A: their cortical EEG is indicative of almost continuous slow-wave sleep

38. What is the encéphale isolé preparation, and how does it seem to sleep?

39. What three early findings supported the reticular-activating theory of sleep?

40.   A: most neurons decrease their activity by no more than 10% during SWS, and during REM sleep many are even more active than during relaxed wakefulness

41. What evidence suggests that there is a sleep-promoting circuit in the caudal brain stem?

42. What evidence is there that various sleep-stage correlates of sleep are dissociable?

43.   A: a cluster of serotonin-producing nuclei running in a thin
                                       strip down the center of the caudal reticular formation

44. What evidence implicates the raphé nuclei in sleep?

45.   A: parachlorophenylalanine

46.   A: basal forebrain region

47. What is the nature of the REM-sleep circuit of the caudal
    brain stem?

48.   A: circadian clock

49.   A: suprachiasmatic nuclei

50. What evidence proves that the SCN contain an important
    circadian timing mechanism?

51. How did Ralph et al. (1990) use the neurotransplantation
    procedure to study the SCN?

52.   A: retinohypothalamic tracts

53.   A: benzodiazepines

54. What is 5-HTP?

55.   A: they are catecholamines

56. What is the mechanism of action of stimulant drugs?

57. Why is stimulant-drug therapy a risky proposition?

58.   A: delta sleep-inducing peptide

59. How was DSIP discovered?

60.   A: parabiotic preparation

61. Sleep disorders fall into two complementary categories.
     What are they?

62. Why do some people complain of sleep disorders when
     their sleep is normal?

63.   A: many cases are iatrogenic

64. How can tolerance and withdrawal symptoms contribute
    to the development of insomnia?

65. What is sleep apnea?

66.   A: nocturnal myoclonus

67. How do restless legs produce insomnia?

68. What was the concept of pseudoinsomnia? Why was it
    abandoned?

    _____

69.   A: narcolepsy

70.   A: it is a sudden loss of muscle tone with no loss of
                                       consciousness; a common symptom of narcolepsy

71. What evidence suggests that narcolepsy is a disorder of
    REM sleep?

72.   A: nucleus magnocellularis

73. What evidence has implicated the nucleus magnocellularis in cataplexy?

74. What do objective studies of long-term sleep reduction indicate?

75. What lines of evidence suggest that 5 1/2 hours sleep is sufficient for most people?

Once you have completed the jeopardy study items, study them. Practice bidirectional studying; make sure that you know the correct answer to every question and the correct question for every answer.

II.   Essay Study Questions

Using Chapter 12 of BIOPSYCHOLOGY, write an outline of the answer to each of the following essay study questions.

1. Describe the five stages of sleep EEG and their relation to EMG and EOG changes.

2. Describe chronologically the events of a typical undisturbed night's sleep.

3. List five common beliefs about sleep and dreaming and what REM-sleep research has had to say about them.

4. Describe the recuperative and circadian theories of sleep.

5. Discuss the factors that play a role in the mammalian circadian sleep-wake cycle?

6. Describe three predictions of the recuperation theory of sleep and the corresponding three predictions of the circadian theory. Evaluate these pairs of hypotheses in the light of the existing experimental evidence.

7. Perhaps sleep is not fundamentally recuperative or circadian; perhaps it is a combination of both. Describe the combined recuperative-circadian model of sleep. What evidence is there that the recuperative function may be filled specifically by slow-wave sleep?

8. Describe the early experiments on the cerveau isolé and the encéphale isolé preparations. What theory of sleep did they suggest?

9. Describe findings that have implicated the suprachiasmatic nuclei and the retinohypothalamic tracts in the timing of circadian sleep-wake cycles.

10. Describe and briefly discuss four different causes of insomnia: sleeping pills, sleep apnea, myoclonus, and restless legs.

When you have answered the essay study questions, memorize your outlines to prepare for your upcoming examination.

III. Practice Examination

After completing most of your studying of Chapter 12, but at least 24 hours before your formal examination, write the following practice examination.

A. Multiple-Choice Section. Circle the correct answer for each question; *REMEMBER that some questions may have more than one correct answer.*

1. K complexes and sleep spindles are characteristic of

    a. stage 1 sleep.
    b. stage 2 sleep.
    c. stage 3 sleep.
    d. stage 4 sleep.

2. Delta waves occur during

    a. stage 1 sleep.
    b. stage 2 sleep.
    c. stage 3 sleep.
    d. stage 4 sleep.

3. REMs typically occur during

   a. stage 1 sleep EEG.
   b. emergent stage 1 sleep EEG.
   c. initial stage 1 sleep EEG.
   d. stage 4 sleep EEG.

4. It is possible to shorten or lengthen circadian cycles by adjusting

   a. the free-running period.
   b. the duration of the light-dark cycle.
   c. zeitgebers.
   d. physical and mental exertion.

5. The free-running circadian clock

   a. is always fast.
   b. is always slow.
   c. is always right on time.
   d. tends to be slow.

6. The simultaneous existence of two different free-running periods in one organism

   a. suggests that there may be more than one circadian timing mechanism.
   b. is supported by the observation of internal desynchronization.
   c. can be observed in subjects housed in constant environmental conditions.
   e. none of the above

7. Randy Gardner stayed awake for

   a. 4 days.
   b. 6 days.
   c. 7 days.
   d. 11 days.

8. Which of the following is not a line of evidence that supports the idea that it is delta sleep, rather than sleep in general, that serves a recuperative function?

   a. Sleep deprived subjects regain almost all of their lost stage 4 sleep.
   b. Subjects who reduce their sleep times do so by reducing the amount of stage 3 and 4 sleep.
   c. Short sleepers get as much stage 3 and stage 4 sleep as long sleepers.
   d. Extra morning naps contain almost no stage 3 or stage 4 sleep, and they don't reduce the duration of the next night's sleep.

9. The current clinical hypnotics of choice are

   a. tricyclic antidepressants.
   b. stimulants.
   c. benzodiazepines.
   d. barbiturates.

10. Which of the following is a cause of insomnia that wakes the patient up many times each night although he or she often does not remember the awakenings in the morning?

    a. sleep apnea
    b. restless legs
    c. myoclonus
    d. narcolepsy

B. Modified True-False and Fill-in-the Blank Section. If the statement is true, write TRUE in the blank provided. If the statement is false, write FALSE as well as the word or words that will make the statement true if they replaced the highlighted word or words in the original statement. If the statement is incomplete, write the word or words that will complete it.

1. The three standard psychophysiological indices of the stages of sleep are the EEG, the EMG, and the _____.

2. All periods of stage 1 sleep EEG other than initial stage 1 sleep EEG are called _____ stage 1 sleep EEG.

3. Stages 2, 3, and 4 are together referred to as _____ sleep.

4. True or False: External stimuli presented to a dreaming subject are **never** incorporated into the dream?

          A: _____

5. True or False: Dreams run on "**real time**"?

          A: _____

6. Some people claim that they do not dream; is their claim true?

7. Is it true that the size of penile or clitoral erections provide a convenient objective measure of the sexual content of the accompanying dream?

8. True or False: Somnambulism is most likely to occur during **dreaming**.

          A: _____

9. Circadian rhythms in a constant environment are called _____ rhythms; their duration is called the free-running _____.

10. Circadian rhythms are entrained by circadian environmental stimuli called _____.

11. Even under free-running conditions, longer periods of wakefulness tend to be followed by _____ periods of sleep.

12. It is usually more difficult to adapt to phase _____ than to phase _____.

13. It is usually more difficult to adapt to _____ flights than to _____ flights of the same duration and distance.

14. _____ are brief periods during which the eyelids droop and the sleep-deprived subject becomes unresponsive to external stimuli without losing the ability to sit or stand.

15. Sleep-deprived subjects display deficits on _____ tasks that require continuous attentiveness.

16. The effects of long-term sleep deprivation have been studied in rats using the _____ apparatus.

17. Most selective sleep-deprivation studies are studies of _____ deprivation.

18. True or False: **Benzodiazepines** selectively block REM sleep at commonly prescribed clinical doses.

        A: _____

19. The two-process model of sleep integrates the effects of both _____ sleep-promoting factors and deprivation-induced sleep-promoting factors.

Write either "cerveau" or "encéphale," which ever is more relevant, next to each of the following four phrases.

20.   intracollicular section: _____ isolé

21.   almost continuous high-amplitude, slow-wave EEG: _____ isolé

22.   alternating periods of wakefulness and sleep EEG: _____ isolé

23.   transection of the caudal brain stem: _____ isolé

24. According to the first major active theory of sleep, sleep resulted from low levels of activity in the so-called _____ system.

25. It has been hypothesized that there are sleep-promoting circuits in the serotonergic _____ nuclei, in other nuclei of the caudal brain stem, and in the basal _____ region.

26. The major circadian timing mechanism appears to be in the _____ nuclei.

27. Visual zeitgebers entrain circadian rhythms through signals carried by the _____ tracts.

28. Research on the mechanisms of cataplexy have linked it to _____ sleep and the cells of the _____.

29. True or False: Insomnia that is caused by prescribed sleeping pills is said to be **iatrogenic**.

        A: _____

30. A withdrawal effect of most sleep-promoting drugs is _____.

31. People who take sleeping pills typically become _____ to their soporific (sleep-promoting) effects, and thus they take larger and larger doses of them.

32. In some cases of sleep _____, spasms of the throat muscles block air intake many times each night.

33. At one time, people complaining of insomnia who were found to sleep more than 6.5 hours per night were labeled _____ and were assumed to be neurotic.

34. _____ a disorder that is often associated with narcolepsy.

C. Short Answer Section. In no more than 4 sentences, answer each of the following questions.

1. Describe the two theories that account for why we sleep. How does Borb9ly (1984) deal with the existence of two theories?

2. Describe what is known about genetic regulation of circadian rhythms.

3. Describe the experiments that led to the discovery of the retinohypothalamic tracts.

4. Describe the three most important findings about the neural basis of sleep that followed the discovery of the reticular activating system.

Mark your answers to the practice examination; the correct answers follow. On the basis of your performance, plan the final stages of your studying.

Answers to Practice Examination

A. Multiple Choice Section

1. b
2. c; d
3. b
4. b; c
5. d

6. a; b; c
7. d
8. b
9. c
10. b; c

B. Modified True/False and Fill-in-the-Blank Section

1. EOG
2. emergent
3. slow-wave
4. False; often
5. True
6. no
7. no
8. False; stage 4
9. free-running; period
10. zeitgebers
11. shorter
12. advances; delays
13. eastern; western
14. Microsleeps
15. boring (or equivalent)
16. carousel
17. REM
18. tricyclic antidepressants

19. circadian
20. cerveau
21. cerveau
22. encéphale
23. encéphale
24. reticular activating
25. raphé; forebrain
26. suprachiasmatic
27. retinohypothalamic
28. REM; nucleus magnocellularis
29. True
30. insomnia
31. tolerant
32. apnea
33. pseudoinsomniacs
34. Cataplexy

C. Short Answer Section

1. Mention the recuperation theories and the circadian theories; the integrated theory of Borbély.

2. Mention per, tau, and clock; the disruption in circadian rhythm produced by mutations of tau and clock.

3. Mention the optic nerves, optic chiasm, optic tracts; the disruption in circadian rhythm produced by cuts placed before or after the optic chiasm.

4. Mention that sleep is not a state of neural quiescence; there are sleep-promoting circuits in the brain; the various correlates of sleep are dissociable.

Chapter 13

DRUG ABUSE AND REWARD CIRCUITS IN THE BRAIN

I.   Jeopardy Study Items

With reference to Chapter 13 of BIOPSYCHOLOGY, write the correct answer to each of the following questions and the correct question for each of the following answers.

1. When were most of the laws governing drug abuse enacted?

2.   A: by ingestion, injection, inhalation, or absorption through mucous membranes

3.   A: SC, IM, IV

4. Which route of drug administration comes to be preferred by many chronic drug addicts? Why?

5. What is drug metabolism?

6. In what two ways can tolerance be demonstrated?

7.   A: in short, it is a shift in the dose-response curve to the right

8.   A: it is called reverse tolerance

9. What is metabolic tolerance?

10. What is functional tolerance?

11.   A: drug withdrawal syndrome

12.   A: they are said to be physically dependent

13. What is the difference between addiction, physical dependence, and psychological dependence?

14. What is a before-and-after design?

15.   A: it is used in most demonstrations of contingent drug tolerance

16. What is the drug-effect theory of tolerance?

17. A: it is called the situational specificity of drug tolerance

18. What is Siegel's theory of conditioned tolerance?

19. What is a conditioned compensatory response?

20. A: next to caffeine, it is the most widely used psychoactive drug

21. Are heavy cigarette smokers addicts?

22. What are the long-term consequences of smoking tobacco?

23. What is Buerger's disease, and what point does it make about the addiction potential of tobacco?

24. A: it is euphemistically referred to as a hangover

25. What are the symptoms of the alcohol withdrawal
    syndrome?

26.   A: Korsakoff's syndrome, cirrhosis of the liver, heart attack,
                                       and gastritis, for example

27.   A: the fetal alcohol syndrome

28. What is delta-9-THC?

29.   A: because they are subtle, difficult to measure, and greatly
                                       influenced by the social situation

30. What are the hazards of long-term marijuana use?

31.   A: lowered plasma testosterone levels, weakened immune
                                       system, cardiovascular problems, and amotivational syndrome

32. What is cocaine hydrochloride?

33.   A: caffeine, cocaine, amphetamine, and nicotine

34. What are cocaine sprees?

35. What is the relation between opium, morphine, codeine, and heroin?

36.   A: as analgesics, in the treatment of diarrhea, and in the treatment of cough

37. Three events prior to the late 1800s fanned the flame of opiate addiction. What were they?

38. What is the Harrison's Narcotic Act, and how did it increase heroin addiction?

39. What are the <u>direct</u> health hazards of opiate addiction?

40. Opiate withdrawal is one of the most misunderstood aspects of drug use. Why?

41.   A: poverty, poor medical care, poor diet, arrest, AIDS, and death from overdose, for example

42. There are serious problems with the system of drug control that is used in many countries. What are they?

43. What is the physical-dependence theory of addiction?

44.   A: by postulating that withdrawal effects can be elicited by conditional stimuli

45. What are two problems with the theory that conditioned withdrawal effects motivate relapse?

46.   A: needle freaks

47. What is the positive-incentive theory of addiction?

48. Why is the intracranial self-stimulation phenomenon of interest to those searching for the neural basis of addiction?

49.   A: priming

50.   A: the mesotelencephalic dopamine system

51.   A: substantia nigra and ventral tegmental area

52. What is 6-hydroxydopamine?

53. What are consummatory behaviors and preparatory
behaviors?

54. What is the conditioned-place-preference paradigm?
What is its main advantage?

55.   A: Song of Praise

Once you have completed the jeopardy study items, study them. Practice bidirectional studying; make sure that you know the correct answer to every question and the correct question for every answer.

II.   Essay Study Questions

Using Chapter 13 of BIOPSYCHOLOGY, write an outline of the answer to each of the following essay study questions.

1. Explain with the aid of a graph that drug tolerance is a shift in the dose-response curve to the right.

2. Drug tolerance effects and drug withdrawal effects are commonly assumed to be different manifestations of the same physiological changes. Explain.

3. What is contingent drug tolerance? Describe an example. Explain how demonstrations of contingent drug tolerance support the drug-effect theory of tolerance.

4. What is the situational specificity of drug tolerance? Describe an example. Describe the conditioned-tolerance theory proposed by Siegel and his colleagues to account for it.

5. Compare the direct health hazards of tobacco, alcohol, marijuana, cocaine, and heroin. On the basis of this comparison, rank them in order of dangerousness.

6. Discuss common misconceptions about drug abuse and common misconceptions about the best way of dealing with the drug-abuse problem.

7. Compare the physical-dependence theory of addiction with the positive-incentive theory of addiction.

8. Describe the main features of the intracranial self-stimulation phenomenon.

9. What is the evidence that the mesotelencephalic dopamine system plays an important role in intracranial self-stimulation?

10. What is the evidence that the mesotelencephalic dopamine system is involved in addiction to opiates and stimulants?

When you have answered the essay study questions, memorize your outlines to prepare for your upcoming examination.

III. Practice Examination

After completing most of your studying of Chapter 13, but at least 24 hours before your formal examination, write the following practice examination.

A. Multiple-Choice Section. Circle the correct answer for each question; *REMEMBER that some questions may have more than one correct answer.*

1. A major advantage and major disadvantage of the oral route of drug administration relative to other routes are:

   a. ease and unpredictability, respectively.
   b. safety and unpredictability, respectively.
   c. predictability and safety, respectively.
   d. speed and unpredictability, respectively.

2. The actions of most drugs in the central nervous system are terminated by:

   a. elimination.
   b. metabolism.
   c. diffusion.
   d. the blood brain barrier.

3. Functional tolerance is due to:

   a. a decrease in the amount of drug getting to its sites of action
   b. a shift in the dose-response curve to the left.
   c. a decrease in reactivity of the sites of action to the drug.
   d. increased metabolism of the drug.

4. Withdrawal syndromes:

   a. indicate a state of physical dependency on the drug.
   b. vary in severity depending on the drug.
   c. vary in severity depending on the speed of drug elimination.
   c. are typically characterized by effects that are opposite to those of the drug.

5. The before-and-after design is used to study:

   a. metabolic tolerance.
   b. contingent tolerance.
   c. conditioned tolerance.
   d. situation-specific tolerance.

6. A current hypothesis is that many of the tobacco-related disorders occur as a result of the presence of _____ in tobacco.

   a. nicotine
   b. tar
   c. free radicals
   d. solvents

7. Chronic exposure to alcohol can produce:

    a. functional tolerance.
    b. metabolic tolerance.
    c. brain damage.
    d. physical dependence.

8. One of the difficulties in characterizing the effects of marijuana is that:

    a. a pure form of the active ingredient is not available.
    b. the active ingredient does not bind to a specific receptor in the brain.
    c. they are subtle
    d. they are greatly influenced by social situation

9. Cocaine exerts its behavioral effects by:

    a. interacting with catecholamine receptors.
    b. increasing reuptake of catecholamines.
    c. decreasing reuptake of catecholamines.
    d. none of the above

10. Opiates are extremely effective in the treatment of:

    a. pain
    b. cough
    c. diarrhea
    d. glaucoma

11. Evidence against the physical-dependence theory of addiction includes the observation that:

    a. detoxified addicts often return to former drug-taking habits.
    b. highly addictive drugs, such as alcohol, produce severe withdrawal distress.
    c. highly addictive drugs, such as cocaine, do not produce severe withdrawal distress.
    d. the pattern of drug taking displayed by many addicts involves periods of detoxification.

12. Early research led to the theory that reinforcement is mediated by activation of the:

    a. nigrostriatal bundle.
    b. fornix.
    c. mesotelencephalic dopamine system.
    d. frenulum.

13. In one well known experiment, unilateral injections of 6-OHDA into the mesotelencephalic dopamine system:

    a. increased self-stimulation from ipsilateral brain sites.
    b. increased self-stimulation from contralateral brain sites.
    c. decreased self-stimulation from contralateral brain sites.
    d. decreased self-stimulation from ipsilateral sites.

14. Two of the following lines of evidence have suggested that the rewarding effects of opiates are mediated by the mesotelencephalic dopamine system. Which two?

    a. Rats lever press for microinjections of opiates into the ventral tegmental area or nucleus accumbens.
    b. Dopamine antagonists block the conditioned place preference normally produced by opiates.
    c. Dopamine agonists block the conditioned place preference normally produced by opiates.
    d. Rats lever press for electrical stimulation of the mesotelencephalic dopamine system.

15. Which of the following has been shown to block the rewarding effects of intravenous stimulants in experiments on laboratory animals?

        a. dopamine antagonists
        b. norepinephrine antagonists
        c. norepinephrine agonists
        d. dopamine agonists

B. Modified True-False and Fill-in-the Blank Section. If the statement is true, write TRUE in the blank provided. If the statement is false, write FALSE as well as the word or words that will make the statement true if they replaced the highlighted word or words in the original statement. If the statement is incomplete, write the word or words that will complete it.

What do the following abbreviations stand for?

1.   IM: _____

2.   IV: _____

3.   SC: _____

4. _____ is a common drug of abuse that is usually self-administered through the mucous membranes.

5. True or False: Tolerance is a shift in the dose-response curve to the **left**.

        A: _____

6. Individuals who suffer withdrawal reactions when they stop taking a drug are said to be _____ on the drug.

7. In one study, tolerance did not develop to the anticonvulsant effect of alcohol unless _____ was administered during the periods of alcohol exposure.

8. According to Siegel, _____ responses become conditioned to environments in which drug effects are repeatedly experienced, and they increasingly offset the effects of the drug, thus producing tolerance.

Next to each of the following phrases write the name of the relevant drug.

9.   major active ingredient of tobacco: _____

10.   major active ingredient of opium: _____

11.   major active ingredient of marijuana: _____

12.   the cause of Buerger's disease: _____

13.   lung cancer, emphysema, bronchitis: _____

14.   Hashishin-i-Sabbah: _____

15.   Korsakoff's syndrome: _____

16.   amotivational syndrome: _____

17.   alleviates glaucoma and nausea: _____

18.   crack: _____

19.   diuretic: _____

20.   soldier's disease: _____

21.   Coca Cola: _____

22.   Dalby's Carminative: _____

23.   gold turkey and goose flesh: _____

24.   reverse tolerance, sprees, psychosis: _____

25.   cirrhosis: _____

26.   morphine, codeine, heroin: _____

27.   delirium tremens: _____

28. True or False: According to the **positive-incentive** theory of addiction, addicts become trapped in a vicious circle of drug taking and withdrawal symptoms.

            A: _____

Which of the following is related to the intracranial self stimulation phenomenon and which is not?

29.   slow extinction   yes ___   no ___

30.   priming   yes ___   no ___

31.   high response rates   yes ___   no ___

32.   Olds and Milner   yes ___   no ___

33. Supporting the theory that ascending dopamine projections play a major role in intracranial self-stimulation is the finding that positive mesencephalic ICSS sites are localized in the substantia nigra and in the

        _____ .

34. True or False: The incentive value of a drug can be measured in laboratory animals in the **place preference conditioning** paradigm, unconfounded by other effects of the drug on behavior.

            A: _____

35. True or False: During his life, the famous psychoanalyst Sigmund Freud used two hazardous drugs. He became seriously addicted to **nicotine** but not to **cocaine**.

            A: _____

Chapter 13

C. Short Answer Section. In no more than 4 sentences, answer each of the following questions.

1. Describe drug tolerance and three important points about the specificity of drug tolerance.

2. Describe the relation between addiction, withdrawal and physical dependence.

3 Describe the drug-effect theory of tolerance and provide one example of tolerance that supports this model.

4. Describe situational specific drug tolerance and provide one example of tolerance that supports this model.

5. Describe the physical-dependence theories of addition and explain how these theories attempt to account for the fact that addicts frequently relapse after lengthy drug-free periods?

6. Describe the positive-incentive theories of addiction. Indicate what two such theories have predicted about the positive-incentive value of addictive drugs with continued drug use.

7. What is the neural substrate of intracranial self-stimulation? List the four types of studies that have provided support for the view that this system of neurons is involved in intracranial self-stimulation.

8. Initially the mesotelencephalic dopamine system was thought to play a role in at least two different phases of natural motivated behaviors. What are these phases? On the basis of current evidence, which of these two phases is now thought to be regulated by the mesotelencephalic dopamine system?

9. Describe the drug self-administration paradigm and the conditioned place-preference paradigm. What is the major advantage of the conditioned place-preference paradigm?

10. Below is a saggital drawing of the rat mesotelencephalic dopamine system. Identify the following structures: ventral tegental area, substantia nigra, nucleus accumbens, striatum, prefrontal cortext, and hippocampus.

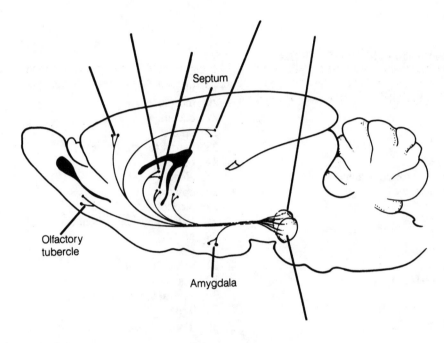

Septum

Olfactory
tubercle

Amygdala

Mark your answers to the practice examination; the correct answers follow. On the basis of your performance, plan the final stages of your studying.

Answers to Practice Examination

A. Multiple Choice Section

1. a, b
2. b
3. c
4. a, b, c, d
5. c
6. a, b, c, d
7. c, d
8. c

9. a, b, c
10. a, c, d
11. b
12. c
13. d
14. a, b
15. a

B. Modified True/False and Fill-in-the-Blank Section

1. intramuscular
2. intravenous
3. subcutaneous
4. cocaine
5. False: right
6. physically dependent
7. convulsive stimulation (or equivalent)
8. conditioned compensatory
9. nicotine
10. morphine
11. delta-9-THC
12. nicotine (or tobacco)
13. nicotine (or tobacco)
14. hashish (or delta-9-THC)
15. alcohol
16. marijuana (or delta-9-THC)
17. marijuana (or delta-9-THC)
18. cocaine

19. alcohol
20. morphine
21. cocaine
22. opium
23. heroin (or morphine)
24. cocaine
25. alcohol
26. opiates
27. alcohol
28. False: physical-dependence
29. no
30. yes
31. yes
32. yes
33. ventral tegmental area
34. True
35. True

C. Short Answer Section

1. Mention that tolerance is a shift in the dose-response curve to the right; cross tolerance; tolerance develops to some effects of the drug but not others; tolerance is not subserved by a single mechanism.

2. Mention that addiction is not related to either withdrawal or physical dependence; withdrawal indicates physical dependence.

3. Mention that tolerance is an adaptation to drug effects, rather than to drug exposure per se; before-and-after experimental design; prove an example such as contingent tolerance to the anticonvulsant effects of alcohol.

4. Mention that a subject may be tolerant to a drug when it is experienced in its usual environment but not when it is experienced in another; provide an example such as conditioned tolerance to the hypothermic effects of alcohol.

5. Mention the vicious circle of drug taking and withdrawal symptoms; these theories postulate that withdrawal symptoms can be elicited by conditional stimuli and as a result addicts may relapse after detoxification.

6. Mention that the primary reason most addicts take drugs is to obtain their pleasurable effects; the positive-incentive value of drugs will increase either because more conditioned tolerance develops to their aversive effects than their pleasurable effects or sensitization develops to their positive incentive value.

7. Mention the mesotelencephalic dopamine system; list mapping studies, microdialysis studies, dopamine agonist and antagonist studies, and lesion studies.

8. Mention consummatory behaviors and preparatory behaviors; the former complete a sequence of motivated behavior (i.e., copulation) whereas the latter enable an organism to perform a consummatory response (i.e., approaching a sex partner); mesotelencephalic dopamine is thought to play a role in consummatory behavior.

9. Mention lever pressing, intravenous catheter, drug compartment, control compartment, test phase; in the conditioned place preference paradigm, subjects are tested drug-free.

10. See Figure 13.4 in BIOPSYCHOLOGY.

11. See Figure 13.8 in BIOPSYCHOLOGY.

Chapter 14

MEMORY AND AMNESIA

I.   Jeopardy Study Items

With reference to Chapter 14 of BIOPSYCHOLOGY, write the correct answer to each of the following questions and the correct question for each of the following answers.

1.   A: the brain's ability to stored the learned effects of its experience.

2.   A: engram

3. Define the principle of mass action and the principle of equipotentiality, respectively?

4.   A: mnemonic

5. What is memory consolidation?

6. Describe Hebb's theory of the consolidation of memory?

7. What was the most important prediction made from
   Hebb's theory of memory consolidation?

8. What is a bilateral medial temporal lobectomy?

9.   A: lobectomy and lobotomy, respectively

10.   A: anterograde and retrograde amnesia, respectively

11. What is H.M.'s most devastating memorial problem?

12.   A: amnesia for information presented in all modalities

13. Why was H.M. able to perform the verbal matching-to-
    sample task, but not the nonverbal form of the task?

14.   A: the mirror-drawing task

15. Describe H.M.'s performance on the following memory tests; when a description of his performance is already given, name the test.

    a. digit span +1 test:

    b.   A: his performance on this version of the block-tapping memory-span test was very poor

    c. verbal and nonverbal matching-to-sample tests

    d.   A: on each trial, he went outside the boundaries less frequently, but he had no recollection of previously performing the task

    e. rotary-pursuit task

    f. incomplete-pictures Test

    g.   A: after 2 years, H.M. performed this task almost perfectly

16. What is the difference between explicit, or declarative, memory and implicit, or procedural, memory?

17. What are the two major subcortical structures of the medial temporal lobes?

18. How did H.M.'s case argue against the notion that each part of the forebrain participates equivalently in the storage of memory?

19.   A: this theory was supported by the fact that H.M.'s surgery abolished the formation of certain kinds of long-term memories while leaving his short-term memorial abilities intact

20. How long was H.M.'s gradient of retrograde amnesia? What did the length of this gradient suggest about the neural basis of consolidation?

21. Why is patient R.B. so significant to the idea that hippocampal damage produces memory deficits?

22. What is Korsakoff's syndrome?

23.   A: medial diencephalon

24. What is repetition priming?

25. What is the anatomical basis of the memory loss that is observed in patients with Korsakoff's syndrome?

26.   A: N.A. and B.J.

27. How is memory impaired following damage to the prefrontal cortex?

28. What is release from proactive interference?

29.   A: neurofibrils, amyloid plaques, and neural degeneration

30. What evidence links cholinergic dysfunction to Alzheimer's disease?

31.   A: nucleus basalis of Meynert, diagonal band of Broca, and medial septal nucleus

32.   A: nootropics

33. What is the most common cause of amnesia? What is this kind of amnesia called?

34.   A: islands of memory

35. What is ECS?

36. How was a gradient of ECS-produced retrograde amnesia demonstrated in rats following one-trial learning?

37. How did Squire and his colleagues demonstrate long gradients of retrograde amnesia in human patients after ECS?

38.   **A:** the nonrecurring-items delayed nonmatching-to-sample task

39. What cortical area seems to play a critical role in the amnesiac effects of medial temporal lobe lesions?

40. What is the Mumby box?

41. Describe how Mumby and his colleagues convincingly demonstrated hippocampal damage caused by may not be the main factor in medial-temporal-lobe amnesia.

42. What kinds of memories are most consistently impaired in rats with hippocampal damage?

43.   **A:** Morris maze and radial arm maze

44. What is the difference between working and reference memory?

45. What is the cognitive-map theory of hippocampal function?

46.   A: place cells

47. What are two alternatives to the cognitive-map theory of
     hippocampal function?

48. Describe the memory deficits of monkeys with prefrontal
     damage.

49. According to current theories, where are memories
     stored?

50.   A: plays a specific role in memory for the emotional
                                          significance of experiences.

51. Describe the role of the cerebellum in memory for the
     conditioned eye-blink response.

52.   A: the position of the reward alternates from trial to trial...

53. What suggests that the dorsomedial nuclei and the medial
     temporal lobes may be components of the same memory
     circuit?

54.   A: pyrithiamine

Once you have completed the jeopardy study items, study them. Practice bidirectional studying; make sure that you know the correct answer to every question and the correct question for every answer.

II.　　Essay Study Questions

Using Chapter 14 of BIOPSYCHOLOGY, write an outline of the answer to each of the following essay study questions.

1.　Describe H.M.'s surgery and summarize the effects that it had on his performance of various tests of memory.

2.　What six important ideas about the biopsychology of memory are, to a large degree, a legacy of H.M.'s case?

3.　What did the case of patient N.A. tell researchers about the importance of the *medial temporal lobes* to the neural bases of memory.

4. There are two memory deficits observed in Korsakoff's syndrome that are believed to result from prefrontal damage. What are they, and what is the evidence for this view?

5. Describe the anterograde and retrograde amnesia observed after a closed-head injury. What does the nature of these disturbances suggest about memory?

6. Describe the nonrecurring-items delayed nonmatching-to-sample task. What evidence is there that it can be used to model human brain-damage-produced amnesia in both monkeys and rats?

7. What is the cognitive-mapping theory of hippocampal function. What evidence supports it?

8. Describe the role of the hippocampus in object-recognition memory.

9. Compare the memory deficits observed in patients with Alzheimer's disease with those of patient H.M.

10. Compare the memory impairments observed in patients with Korsakoff's syndrome with the impairments observed in H.M. What do the difference tell us about the neural basis of memory?

11. Compare the cognitive-map theory, the configural association theory, and the declarative memory theory of hippocampal function.

12. Describe the pathology that accompanies Alzheimer's disease; in particular, which transmitter systems are compromised in patients with this disease?

When you have answered the essay study questions, memorize your outlines to prepare for your upcoming examination.

III. Practice Examination

After completing most of your studying of Chapter 14, but at least 24 hours before your formal examination, write the following practice examination.

A. Multiple-Choice Section. Circle the correct answer for each question; *REMEMBER that some questions may have more than one correct answer.*

1. According to Hebb's two-stage theory of memory storage, short-term memories were stored by:

   a. consolidation.
   b. reverberating neural activity.
   c. long-term memories.
   d. synaptic disinhibition.

2. A deficit in retrieval of information that was learned before an accident represents a case of:

   a. consolidation.
   b. ischemia.
   c. retrograde amnesia.
   d. explicit memory.

3. H.M.'s operation involved bilateral removal of:

   a. the hippocampus.
   b. the dorsal-medial nucleus of the thalamus.
   c. the amygdala.
   d. the prefrontal cortex.

4. In terms of its effect on his epilepsy, H.M.'s bilateral medial temporal lobectomy was:

   a. a modest failure.
   b. a modest success.
   c. an unqualified success.
   d. a dismal failure.

5. After his operation, H.M. had:

   a. a mild retrograde amnesia for the events of the year or two preceding surgery.
   b. a severe anterograde amnesia.
   c. a severe retrograde amnesia for remote events (e.g., the events of his childhood).
   d. a mild anterograde amnesia.

6. H.M.'s ability to perform tests of short-term memory (e.g., the digit span test) are:

    a. nonexistent.
    b. severely disturbed.
    c. severely disturbed, but only some of the time.
    d. reasonably normal.

7. Which of the following statements about H.M.'s case is not true? H.M.'s case

    a. was one of the first to implicate the medial- temporal lobes in memory.
    b. strongly challenged the view that there are two physiologically distinct modes of storage for short-term and long-term memory.
    c. was among the first clear demonstrations of the survival of implicit long-term memory in an amnesic subject.
    d. showed that gradients of retrograde amnesia could cover very long periods of time.

8. An autopsy revealed that R.B. had ischemia-produced damage to the:

    a. hippocampus.
    b. pyramidal cell layer.
    c. CA1 subfield.
    d. amygdala

9. Evidence suggests that the amnesic symptoms of Korsakoff's syndrome are largely attributable to damage to the:

    a. mediodorsal nuclei.
    b. cortex.
    c. hippocampus.
    d. temporal stem.

10. N.A. suffers from a:

    a. large ischemia-produced infarction.
    b. bilateral thalamic lesion.
    c. lesion that included one mediodorsal nucleus.
    d. lesion that is restricted to one mediodorsal nucleus.

11. Evidence suggests that some of the memory deficits of Korsakoff patients are attributable to prefrontal damage. These memory deficits include their:

    a. failure to release from proactive interference.
    b. inability to form implicit memories.
    c. poor memory for temporal sequence.
    d. deficits on delayed matching-to-sample tasks.

12. In patients with Alzheimer's disease, there is:

    a. a major selective reduction in dopamine.
    b. less choline acetyltransferase.
    c. less acetylcholinesterase.
    d. a major reduction in cholinergic receptors.

13. After his electroconvulsive therapy, Craig did not remember any thing about his week of hospitalization except Carolyn's visit on the third day. This recollection is:

    a. short-term memory.
    b. an island of memory.
    c. an implicit memory.
    d. hypermetaamnesia.

14. In a series of studies of amnesia for television shows, Squire and his colleagues found a gradient of retrograde amnesia in patients after electroconvulsive therapy; the gradient was about:

    a. 1 minute long.
    b. 5 minutes long.
    c. 1 hour long.
    d. 2 years long.

15. According to the configural-association theory of hippocampal function, the hippocampus:

    a. is responsible for the memories of individual stimuli.
    b. is responsible for memories of the relationships between stimuli.
    c. is best able to describe the effects of hippocampal lesions on the performance of rats in a Morris water maze.
    d. has a role in the formation of all explicit memories.

16. Monkeys with prefrontal cortex lesions displayed memory deficits on the:

    a. nonrecurring-items delayed nonmatching-to-sample test.
    b. recurring-items delayed matching-to-sample test.
    c. delayed-alternation test.
    d. a and c

17. Which of the following is an area of the medial-temporal lobe?

    a. entorhinal cortex
    b. hippocampus
    c. amygdala
    d. mammillary bodies

B. Modified True-False and Fill-in-the Blank Section. If the statement is true, write TRUE in the blank provided. If the statement is false, write FALSE as well as the word or words that will make the statement true if they replaced the highlighted word or words in the original statement. If the statement is incomplete, write the word or words that will complete it.

1. True or False: The term **"lobotomy"** can be used to describe H.M.'s surgery.

   A: _____

2. Assessment of the amnesic effects of bilateral medial-temporal-lobe lesions in animals seems to rule out the theory that _____ damage by itself is responsible for medial-temporal-lobe amnesia.

3. Number these five phases of posttraumatic amnesia from 1 to 5 to indicate their chronological order.

   ___. blow to the head
   ___. period covered by the retrograde amnesia
   ___. period of coma
   ___. period of confusion and anterograde amnesia
   ___. period during which normal memories are formed but there is still retrograde amnesia for the brief period before the blow

4. True or False: The **repetition priming** test that has proven most useful in studying medial-temporal-lobe amnesia in monkeys.

   A: _____

Next to the following seven statements, write the name of one of the following tests: digit span test, digit span +1 test, block-tapping memory-span +1 test, matching-to-sample test, mirror-drawing test, rotary-pursuit test, incomplete-pictures test

5. After 25 trials, H.M. could still only do 7.

   A: _____

6. H.M. did not learn a sequence one more than his normal span when the same sequence was presented 12 times.

   A: _____

7. H.M.'s time-on-target increased over 12 daily sessions although he did not recall them.

   A: _____

8. There are five sets of cards. H.M. showed improvement when the test was unexpectedly repeated an hour later.

   A: _____

9. His score was 6, which is well within the normal range of performance for healthy subjects.

   A: _____

10. H.M. performed better on verbal items than on nonverbal items, such as ellipses.

   A: _____

11. There are several hypotheses about the location of the tissue whose damage is responsible for the amnesia of those with bilateral medial-temporal-lobe lesions. Although initial research focused on the hippocampus, recent evidence from animal studies points to the overlying _____.

12. One interpretation of the gradient of "retrograde amnesia" observed in Korsakoff patients is that it reflects the progressive worsening of _____ amnesia.

13. Some of N.A.'s brain damage was visible on a _____.

14. At autopsy, the brains of Alzheimer patients display three striking forms of pathology: neuronal degeneration, _____ plaques, and _____ in the neural cytoplasm. (2 marks)

15. There is a major reduction in the neurotransmitter, _____ in the brains of Alzheimer patients.

16. Gradients of retrograde amnesia can be studied in laboratory animals by administering _____ to groups of animals at different intervals after a learning trial.

17. The nonrecurring-items delayed nonmatching-to-sample apparatus that was developed for rats is called the _____ box.

18. Much of the research on implicit memory has employed the repetition- _____ task.

19. Squire and his colleagues believe that there are two fundamentally different kinds of memories, procedural memories and _____ memories, which are measured by implicit and explicit tests of memory, respectively.

20. The _____ is the hypothetical change in the brain responsible for storing a memory.

21. The memory deficits observed in patients with Alzheimer's disease or with Korsakoff's syndrome are similar in that there is _____ amnesia in both groups of patients.

22. The _____ is comprised of the entorhinal and perirhinal cortex.

23. In Okeefe and Speakman's "four-arm maze" task, the activity of place cells in the hippocampus suggested that the rats were "guessing" _____ relative to the place field.

24. _____ is a disorder common in people who have consumed large quantities of alcohol for prolonged periods of time.

25. True or False: The **dorsomedial nucleus of the thalamus** is important to memories about the emotional aspects of an experience.

    A: _____

C. Short Answer Section. In no more than 4 sentences, answer each of the following questions.

1. Compare the amnesia associated with bilateral medial-temporal lobectomy and that associated with Korsakoff's syndrome.

2. Describe Lashley's search for the engram, and what his efforts suggested about the neural basis of learning and memory.

Mark your answers to the practice examination; the correct answers follow. On the basis of your performance, plan the final stages of your studying.

Chapter 14

Answers to the Practice Examination

A. Multiple Choice Section

1. b
2. c
3. a, c
4. b
5. a, b
6. d
7. d
8. a, b, c
9. a
10. c
11. a, c
12. b, c
13. b
14. d
15. b
16. b, c
17. a, b, c

B. Modified True/False and Fill-in-the-Blank Section

1. F; lobectomy
2. hippocampal
3. 2, 1, 3, 4, 5
4. F; nonrecurring-items delayed-nonmatching-to-sample
5. digit-span + 1 task
6. block-tapping memory-span
7. rotary-pursuit
8. incomplete-pictures
9. digit-span
10. matching-to-sample test
11. cortex
12. anterograde
13. CAT scan
14. amyloid, neurofibrillary tangles
15. acetylcholine
16. ECS
17. Mumby
18. priming
19. declarative
20. engram
21. retrograde
22. rhinal cortex
23. the location of the reward
24. Korsakoff's syndrome
25. F; amygdala

C. Short Answer Section

1. Mention the fact that Korsakoff's patients have significant retrograde amnesia; that both groups have anterograde amnesia; that Korsakoff's amnesia is due to diencephalic damage, in contrast to temporal-lobe patients.

2. Mention that it looked at the effects of brain lesions on an animal's memory for events prior to the surgery; that it was unsuccessful; that it slowed research in the area of assigning specific functional significance to specific parts of the brain.

3. See Figure 14.19 in BIOPSYCHOLOGY.

Chapter 15

NEUROPLASTICITY: DEVELOPMENT, LEARNING, AND RECOVERY FROM BRAIN DAMAGE

I.   Jeopardy Study Items

With reference to Chapter 15 of BIOPSYCHOLOGY, write the correct answer to each of the following questions and the correct question for each of the following answers.

1. What is the simple systems approach to the study of neuroplasticity? What is its main advantage?

2. In addition to cell multiplication, what three processes are responsible for the development of organisms into distinct entities?

3.   A: the neural plate, the neural groove, and the neural tube

4.   A: forebrain, midbrain, and hindbrain

5. With the development of the neural plate, the cells of the dorsal ectoderm lose their totipotency. What does this mean?

6. What is induction?

7.   A: most occurs in the ventricular zone

8.   A: they migrate along radial glial cells

9. Describe the migration of cells from the ventricular zone to the subventricular, intermediate, and cortical areas.

10.   A: its called the inside-out pattern of cortical development

11. What is the neural crest? Why is it of special interest to scientists who study neural migration?

12. What are neural cell-adhesion molecules?

13.   A: it is thought to be mediated by neural cell-adhesion molecules

14. What is the growth cone? Why is it important to the study of neural development?

15. What is the chemoaffinity hypothesis of axonal development?

16. What experiment led Roger Sperry to propose the
    chemoaffinity hypothesis?

17. Why did Sperry <u>choose</u> the frog's visual system to the
    study of axonal development.

18.   A: They will grow to their normal targets even in a tissue
                                         culture.

19.   A: because it cannot explain why growing axons innervate
                                         inappropriate target sites implanted in the area of the
                                         appropriate target

20. What is the blueprint hypothesis of neural development?

21. How do pioneer growth cones find their targets?

22.   A: fasciculation

23.   A: it cannot explain how some axons grow to their correct
                                         targets after their starting points have been surgically altered

24. What is the topographic-gradient hypothesis?

25.   A: it is always mapped onto the optic tectum, regardless of its
                                         size

26. What three findings suggest that developing neurons die because of their failure to compete successfully for a life-promoting factor from their target?

27.   A: it is taken up by, and promotes the survival of, sympathetic neurons

28. What are two consequences of cell death in the central nervous system?

29.   A: "use it or loose it"

30. How has the impact of early experience on neural development been demonstrated in studies of animals reared in the dark?

31. How has the competitive nature of synapse rearrangement been illustrated in studies of early monocular deprivation?

32. What evidence demonstrates the interaction of auditory and visual topographic maps during neural development?

33. Define learning and memory.

34. How does the Aplysia gill-withdrawal reflex work?

35. Define *nonassociative learning*.

36.   A: it is called habituation

37. What was the first clue about the neural mechanism underlying habituation of the gill withdrawal reflex in *Aplysia*?

38.   A: calcium ions

39.   A: it is called sensitization

40. How does presynaptic facilitation mediate sensitization?

41. What is Pavlovian conditioning, and how has it been demonstrated in Aplysia?

42. What is the difference between sensitization and Pavlovian conditioning?

43.   A: it is called long-term potentiation

44. What are second messengers? Give and example of one second messenger pathway.

45. What is the difference between short-term and long-term
    memories in *Aplysia?*

46.   A: they had fewer active zones, smaller active zones, and
                                           fewer synaptic vesicles

47.   A: it is called long-term potentiation

48. How is the long-term potentiation that is produced by
    perforant path stimulation measured?

49.   A: it can be studied in freely moving or anesthetized animals,
                                           or in hippocampal slices

50. What two characteristics make LTP so useful to Hebb's
    hypothesis about the neural bases of learning and
    memory?

51.   A: Hebb's postulate for learning

52. What six lines of indirect evidence suggest the
    physiological changes underlying LTP may be
    comparable to those that store memories?

53.   A: the NMDA receptor

54. What quality makes the NMDA receptor unique? Why is it important to the induction of LTP?

55. Why is the requirement for postsynaptic neurons to be depolarized when glutamate binds to such an important characteristic of LTP?

56. Why are dendritic spines important to the specificity of LTP?

57.   A: nitric oxide

58.   A: axotomy

59.   A: anterograde and retrograde degeneration

60. Why does anterograde degeneration occur so quickly?

61. What is phagocytosis? What two cell types are responsible for this process?

62. What is required for successful regeneration?

63.   A: collateral sprouting

64. What is the evidence that collateral sprouting is elicited by some factor released by the target tissue?

65.   A: because of their topographic layout

66.   What 3 manipulations can be used to cause the reorganization of sensory cortex.

67. How does motor cortex reorganize itself in adult animals?

68.   A: change in the strength of existing connections or collateral sprouting

69. What three general conclusions have emerged from research on the recovery of function?

70.   A: in the wall of a ventricle, in a surgically created cavity, or it can be broken up and injected into the brain

71. Does transplanted embryonic tissue make connections similar to those that it would have made had it been left in the donor?

72. What are the two strategies adopted for the use of neurotransplantation to treat CNS disorders?

73. Describe the facilitatory effects on neural regeneration of a transplanted "Schwann-cell pipeline".

74. What evidence is there that substantia nigra transplants alleviate Parkinson's disease?

Once you have completed the jeopardy study items, study them. Practice bidirectional studying; make sure that you know the correct answer to every question and the correct question for every answer.

II.   Essay Study Questions

Using Chapter 15 of BIOPSYCHOLOGY, write an outline of the answer to each of the following essay study questions.

1. Describe the five stages of neural development: (1) induction of the neural plate, (2) neural proliferation, (3) migration and aggregation, (4) axon growth and (5) synapse rearrangement.

2. Describe the role that neural death has in the synaptic organization and subsequent function of the nervous system.

3. Compare the evidence for and against the chemoaffinity, blueprint, and topographic-gradient hypotheses.

4. Describe the neural basis of the following kinds of learning in the Aplysia gill-withdrawal circuit: habituation, sensitization, and Pavlovian conditioning.

5. What is LTP, and why are biopsychologists so interested in it? What appear to be the mechanisms of its induction, maintenance, and expression?

6. Describe the various categories of neuronal and transneuronal degeneration.

7. How do adult motor and sensory systems reorganize themselves after damage?

8. Describe the evidence that neurotransplantation might be effective against Parkinson's disease. What is the current status of adrenal medulla autotransplantation?

9. Compare the neural bases of short-term and long-term memory in the gill-withdrawal reflex of *Aplysia*.

10. Our understanding of the mechanisms for the maintenance and expression of long-term potentiation have advanced on three fronts. Comment on each of these areas of research.

When you have answered the essay study questions, memorize your outlines to prepare for your upcoming examination.

III. Practice Examination

After completing most of your studying of Chapter 15, but at least 24 hours before your formal examination, write the following practice examination.

A. Multiple-Choice Section. Circle the correct answer for each question; *REMEMBER that some questions may have more than one correct answer.*

1. Which layer of the neural tube displays the inside-out pattern of development?

     a. cortical plate
     b. intermediate zone
     c. ventricular zone
     d. marginal zone

2. At the tip of each growing axon is :

     a. a synapse.
     b. a structure with filopodia.
     c. a growth cone.
     d. an astrocyte.

3. According to one theory, only pioneer growth cones need to be able to travel to the correct destination; the other growth cones in a developing tract get there by:

     a. festination.
     b. blue prints.
     c. nerve growth factor.
     d. fasciculation.

4. In the newborn cat and monkey, input into layer IV of the primary visual cortex from the two eyes is:

     a. in ocular dominance columns.
     b. in alternating segregated columns.
     c. segregated into alternating stripes about 0.5 millimeter wide.
     d. intermingled

5. In the Pavlovian conditioning of the Aplysia gill-withdrawal reflex, the conditional stimulus is usually:

     a. a noxious stimulus.
     b. a light touch of the siphon.
     c. a strong shock to the tail.
     d. a weak shock to the tail.

6. Stimulation of the perforant path produces a multiple-unit response that is commonly recorded in the:

    a. hippocampus.
    b. hippocampal dentate gyrus.
    c. granule-cell layer.
    d. hippocampal-slice preparation.

7. Despite the difficulties in studying recovery of function, the following general conclusions have emerged:

    a. Recovery of function is less common than is generally believed.
    b. Small lesions are more likely than large lesions to be associated with recovery.
    c. Recovery is more likely in young patients.
    d. Brain damage is not as detrimental to behavior as one might expect.

8. Collateral sprouting is thought to be triggered by some factor released by the:

    a. regenerating axons.
    b. degenerating axons.
    c. target.
    d. growth cones.

9. Many neurons with their cell bodies in the substantia nigra:

    a. release dopamine.
    b. terminate in the striatum.
    c. contribute axons to the nigrostriatal bundle.
    d. die in patients suffering from Parkinson's disease.

10. Transplantation of dopamine-containing cells into the striatum:

    a. is most effective when the cells are derived from adrenal medulla.
    b. is most effective when the cells are derived from an early-term fetus.
    c. has not been effective in the treatment of Parkinson's disease.
    d. has only been successful in nonhuman primates.

B. Modified True-False and Fill-in-the Blank Section. If the statement is true, write TRUE in the blank provided. If the statement is false, write FALSE as well as the word or words that will make the statement true if they replaced the highlighted word or words in the original statement. If the statement is incomplete, write the word or words that will complete it.

1. Why have many researchers interested in neuroplasticity focused on invertebrates and simple vertebrates? The answer in one word is "_____."

2. Write neural tube, neural groove, and neural plate in their correct developmental sequence.

3. Prior to the development of the neural plate, cells of the dorsal ectoderm are _____.

4. The development of the neural plate appears to be induced by the underlying _____.

5. True or False: The <u>subventricular zone</u> of the neural tube contains developing ependymal cells.

> A: _____

6. Glial cells and interneurons develop in the _____ zone of the neural tube.

7. Migrating neurons move outward along _____ cells to their destinations.

8. The assumption that co-occurrence of activity is a physiological necessity for learning is often referred to as _____.

9. True or False: The main guiding force underlying axonal migration appears to the growth cones' attraction to <u>neural cell-adhesion molecules</u> .

> A: _____

10. In frogs, the retinal ganglion cells terminate in the _____.

11. True or False: The <u>chemoaffinity hypothesis</u> can explain why targets transplanted to novel positions become incorrectly innervated.

> A: _____

12. The _____ can account for the fact that axons can grow to their targets when their starting points have been shifted.

13. The _____ can explain how a severed frog retinal ganglion cell regenerates to its original target.

Three lines of evidence support the topographic gradient hypothesis. Complete the following three statements.

14. Axons regenerating from intact frog retinas to lesioned optic tectums _____ _____.

15. Axons regenerating from the remaining portions of lesioned frog retinas to intact optic tectums _____.

16. Synaptic connections between eyes and optic tectums are established long before either reaches full size. As they grow, the initially established synaptic connections _____ _____.

17. The Aplysia gill-withdrawal reflex is commonly elicited in experiments by touching or shocking the _____.

18. Name two types of nonassociative learning.

    a. _____

    b. _____

19. True or False: During **habituation,** the responsiveness of motor neurons to neurotransmitter released by sensory neurons does not decline.

    A: _____

20. During habituation, the number of action potentials elicited in the _____ by each successive touch declines.

21. _____ is a general increase in an animal's responsiveness to stimuli following a noxious stimulus.

22. True or False: **Sensitization** results from a decrease in the amount of neurotransmitter released by the siphon sensory neurons in response to their own action potentials.

    A: _____

23. Pavlovian conditioning of the Aplysia gill-withdrawal reflex can be thought of as a special case of _____.

24. The long-term facilitation of synaptic transmission that underlies LTP is similar in certain respects to the facilitation that has been presumed to be the basis of _____.

25. One important discovery about LTP from the psychological perspective is that it is amenable to _____ conditioning.

26. The _____ receptor is a glutamate receptor subtype that is thought to play an important role in LTP.

27. The _____ of activity in presynaptic and postsynaptic neurons is the critical factor in all forms of associative neural plasticity.

28. Degeneration of the distal segment of an axon is commonly referred to as _____ degeneration.

29. True or false: If CNS tissue is transplanted to a corresponding position in the host, it will **rarely establish** connections with the surrounding tissue.

    A: _____

30. Aguayo and his colleagues have promoted the regeneration of rat CNS neurons by implanting "_____-cell pipelines."

31. Bilateral transplantation of _____ has proven effective in alleviating parkinsonian symptoms in animal models.

32. Injections of _____ into primates causes severe Parkinson's disease.

C. Short Answer Section. In no more than 4 sentences, answer each of the following questions.

1. Two mechanisms have been proposed to account for the reorganization of neural circuits in adult mammals after damage. What are they, and what evidence supports each mechanism?

2. Long-term potentiation and learning and memory processes are phenomenologically similar in eight different ways; describe four areas of similarity.

3. Following axotomy, four different kinds of degeneration occur. They are illustrated in the following figure. Label them.

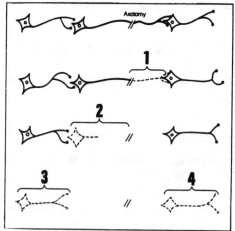

Mark your answers to the practice examination; the correct answers follow. On the basis of your performance, plan the final stages of your studying.

Chapter 15

Answers to the Practice Examination

A. Multiple Choice Section

1. a
2. b, c
3. d
4. d
5. b

6. a, b, c, d
7. a, b, c
8. c
9. a, b, c, d
10. b

B. Modified True/False and Fill-in-the-Blank Section

1. simplicity
2. plate, groove, tube
3. totipotential
4. mesoderm
5. F; ventricular
6. subventricular
7. radial-glial
8. Hebb's postulate
9. F; chemical signals from target structures.
10. optic tectum
11. F; blueprint hypothesis
12. chemoaffinity hypothesis
13. topographic gradient hypothesis
14. squeeze into the space available on the tectum.
15. spread out to fill the space available on the tectum.
16. shift to maintain the topographic map between retina and tectum.

17. siphon
18. habituation; sensitization
19. True
20. gill motor neurons
21. Sensitization
22. F; Habituation
23. sensitization
24. memory
25. associative (or Pavlovian)
26. NMDA
27. co-occurrence
28. anterograde
29. F; typically
30. Schwann
31. fetal substantia nigra cells
32. MPTP

C. Short Answer Section

1. Mention strengthening of existing connections (e.g., reorganization can occur too quickly for new circuits to be formed; this occurs in an area of tissue no more than 2 mm); and new connections due to collateral sprouting (e.g., reorganization can occur over areas of tissue too great to be explained by changes in existing circuitry).

2. Mention 4 of the following: the longevity of LTP and learning/memory; the need for co-occurrence of activity; both can be elicited by low levels of activity; LTP and memory can be elicited in similar neural structures; learning can produce LTP; both phenomena can be altered by similar types of drugs; maximal LTP blocks learning; genetic mutants that display little LTP also have profound learning deficits.

3. See Figure 15.19 in BIOPSYCHOLOGY

Chapter 16

LATERALIZATION, LANGUAGE, AND THE SPLIT BRAIN

I.   Jeopardy Study Items

With reference to Chapter 16 of BIOPSYCHOLOGY, write the correct answer to each of the following questions and the correct question for each of the following answers.

1. What are cerebral commissures?

2.   A: commissurotomy

3. What did Broca discover?

4.   A: although the symptoms are bilateral, this movement
                                                            disorder is usually produced by a left-hemisphere lesion

5.   A: cerebral dominance

6. What is the sodium amytal test?

7. What is the dichotic listening test?

8. Why does the superior ear on the dichotic listening test indicate the dominance of the contralateral hemisphere?

9. Why are words presented in the right visual field recognized more frequently than words presented to the left visual field?

10. Gestures accompanying speech tend to be made with which hand?

11.   A: dextrals or sinestrals

12. What is the relation between handedness and speech laterality for dextrals, sinestrals, and ambidextrous people?

13. Why did McGlone conclude that the brains of males are more lateralized than the brains of females?

14. What was the paradox of the corpus callosum in the early 1950s?

15.   A: by cutting both the corpus callosum and the optic chiasm and blindfolding one eye

16.   A: it produces a scotoma covering the entire medial half of each retina (i.e., in the temporal half of the visual field of each eye)

17. Why is there no transfer of fine tactual and motor information in split-brain monkeys?

18. How can the spread of epileptic discharges be surgically prevented?

19. Why in human split-brain studies are visual stimuli commonly presented for only 0.1 second?

20. Why is the optic chiasm never cut in human split-brain surgery?

21. What was the key difference between split-brain studies done in animals and those done in humans?

22. What evidence supports the idea that the hemispheres of the human brain can function independently?

23. What evidence is there that the two hemispheres of a split-brain patient can learn two different things at the same time?

24.   A: it is called cross-cueing

25. What is the helping-hand phenomenon?

26. How did the results of Levy, Trevarthen, and Sperry's (1972) chimeric-figures-test split-brain experiment support the idea that the two cerebral hemispheres could function independently?

27.   A: it was developed by Zaidel to compare the abilities of the hemispheres of split-brain patients

28. Why is the idea that the left hemisphere is dominant considered obsolete?

29.   A: two disorders of spatial perception associated with damage to the right hemisphere

30.   A: it suggests that emotions, but not visual information, are transferred between hemispheres in split-brain patients

31. Why did Kimura conclude that the right hemisphere was superior for the perception of melodies?

32.   A: planum temporale, Heschel's gyrus, and the frontal operculum

33.   A: it is associated with perfect pitch perception

34. What are the analytic and synthetic modes of thinking?

35. What is Kimura's sensorimotor theory of cerebral lateralization?

36.   A: Wernicke-Geschwind model

37. Where are Broca's and Wernicke's areas?

38.   A: Broca's aphasia and Wernicke's aphasia

39.   A: word salad

40. What is conduction aphasia?

41. What kind of language deficits are produced by damage
     to the left angular gyrus?

42. What is the difference between a serial model and a
     parallel model?

43.   A: are seven components to the Wernicke-Geschwind model

44. According to the Wernicke-Geschwind model, what
     events occur in your cortex when you are having a
     conversation?

45. In general, what effect does damage to various parts of
     the left hemisphere have on language-related abilities?

46. What have CAT and MRI studies told us about the cause
     of language-related disorders?

47. What is a global aphasia?

48.   A: left basal ganglia, left subcortical white matter, or left thalamus

49.   A: phonemes

50. What have brain- stimulation studies suggested about the cortical localization of language?

51.   A: the part of the brain that seems to underlie the phonological analysis of language

52.   A: There are two ways: by a lexical procedure or by a nonlexical procedure

53.   A: dyslexia

54. What kind of clinical condition has lent support to the dual-route model of reading aloud?

55. What is the difference between surface dyslexia and deep dyslexia?

56. What evidence is there that nonlexical language skills are localized to the left hemisphere?

57. What were the three innovations of the blood-flow measurement technique used by Petersen and his colleagues to study language localization?

58.   A: there was no activity in either Wernicke's area or the angular gyrus during visual tests; the semantic processing of verb association occurred in frontal and medial cortex; and there was a great deal of unpredicted activity in the right hemisphere and in the midline areas of both hemispheres

59.   A: the location where semantic processing of verb association appears to occur

60. Describe the shift in the location of processing of verbal information that occurred with practice in the experiments of Petersen and his colleagues.

Once you have completed the jeopardy study items, study them. Practice bidirectional studying; make sure that you know the correct answer to every question and the correct question for every answer.

II.   Essay Study Questions

Using Chapter 16 of BIOPSYCHOLOGY, write an outline of the answer to each of the following essay study questions.

1. What has neuropsychological research suggested about the lateralization of language in humans and its relation to handedness?

2. Discuss the statement "Laterality of function is statistical, not absolute."

3. Using a diagram, describe Myers and Sperry's ground-breaking 1953 experimental study of split-brain cats. What did it suggest?

4. Summarize the results of tests with split-brain patients. What do these results suggest about the function of the corpus callosum and the organization of our brains?

5. What are the two major theories of cerebral asymmetry? Supply one observation to support each.

6. What are the seven components of the Wernicke-Geschwind model? Locate them on a drawing of the left hemisphere. How does the model explain reading aloud?

7. Assess the degree to which the results of various kinds of studies have confirmed the predictions of the Wernicke-Geschwind model.

8. Describe the blood-flow method developed by Petersen and his colleagues to study language localization. Compare their results with the predictions of the Wernicke-Geschwind model.

9. Compare surface and deep dyslexia.

10. Compare the sodium amytal test and the dichotic listening test of language laterality.

11. Describe Penfield's cortical stimulation experiments and the localization of language.

12. What can be learned about the localization of language by studying neuroanatomical asymmetries

When you have answered the essay study questions, memorize your outlines to prepare for your upcoming examination.

III. Practice Examination

After completing most of your studying of Chapter 16, but at least 24 hours before your formal examination, write the following practice examination.

A. Multiple-Choice Section. Circle the correct answer for each question; *REMEMBER that some questions may have more than one correct answer*

1. This unknown country doctor is now recognized as the first to have presented an academic paper on the topic of lateralization of function:

   a. Dax
   b. Broca
   c. Geschwind
   d. Wernicke

2. Which of the following is not normally cut during a conventional commissurotomy performed on a human epileptic?

   a. optic chiasm
   b. anterior commissure
   c. hippocampal commissure
   d. corpus callosum

3. Which of the following did not occur in the ground-breaking 1953 split-brain experiment of Myers and Sperry.

   a. Some cats had their corpus callosums transected.
   b. Some cats had their optic chiasms transected.
   c. All cats were trained to fixate on a point.
   d. Some cats had both their optic chiasms and their corpus callosums transected.

4. The performance of one group of cats fell to 50% at the start of stage two of the ground-breaking experiment of Myers and Sperry. The cats in this group had their:

   a. optic chiasms transected.
   b. corpus callosums transected.
   c. epileptic foci destroyed.
   d. memories impaired.

5. Which of Sperry's colleagues bore the primary responsibility for testing the first group of commissurotomized patients?

   a. Vogel
   b. Bogen
   c. Bryden
   d. Gazzaniga

6. In a well-known study, split-brain patients performed the chimeric figures test. When asked what they had seen, they:

    a. verbally reported seeing whole faces rather than chimeric figures.
    b. verbally reported that they had seen a whole face that was a completed version of the half that had been in their right visual field.
    c. pointed to a whole face that was a completed version of the half that had been in the left visual field.
    d. were confused.

7. In tests of language competence, the right hemisphere of a split-brain subject tends to have:

    a. no language skills.
    b. a completely intact set of language skills that is normally overshadowed by the left hemisphere.
    c. the language skills of a two year old.
    d. the language skills of a preschooler.

8. Damage to which of the following structures has been associated with alexia and agraphia?

    a. angular gyrus
    b. arcuate fasciculus
    c. Broca's area
    d. Wernicke's area

9. Who was a major contributor to the formulation of the Wernicke-Geschwind model?

    a. Wernicke
    b. Geschwind
    c. Dejerine
    d. Broca

10. Small surgical lesions that selectively destroy Broca's area or the angular gyrus, or selectively transect the arcuate fasciculus:

    a. produce Broca's aphasia.
    b. produce conduction aphasia.
    c. have little, if any, lasting effect on language- related abilities.
    d. produce Wernicke's aphasia

11. In a study of 214 patients with brain damage, what proportion was found to have pure Broca's aphasia, and what proportion was found to have pure Wernicke's aphasia?

    a. 90 % and 10 %, respectively
    b. 81 % and 19 %, respectively
    c. 62 % and 38 %, respectively
    d. 0 % and 0 %, respectively

12. In one study, several language tests were administered to conscious patients while they received electrical brain stimulation. It was found that:

    a. the areas of the cortex to which stimulation disrupted test performance extended far beyond the boundaries of the Wernicke-Geschwind areas.
    b. each test was disrupted by both anterior and posterior stimulation.
    c. there were major differences among the subjects in the cortical organization of language.
    d. stimulation at various depths in one column of tissue often disrupted the performance of only a single test.

13. Which of the following is considered to be part of Wernicke's area?

    a. Heschl's gyrus
    b. frontal operculum
    c. planum temporale
    d. angular gyrus

14. In Kimura's tests of musical ability, the right ear/left hemisphere was better able to:

    a. perceive melodies.
    b. perceive digits.
    c. perceive single notes.
    d. perceive complex rhythms.

15. According to Petersen's dual-route theory of language, the performance of a highly practiced verbal response involves:

    a. processing moves from sensory cortex to motor cortex through the association cortex of the lateral fissure.
    b. processing moves from sensory cortex to motor cortex through the frontal and cingulate cortex.
    c. processing moves from sensory cortex to motor cortex through the corpus callosum.
    d. processing moves from sensory cortex to motor cortex through the optic chiasm.

B. Modified True-False and Fill-in-the Blank Section. If the statement is true, write TRUE in the blank provided. If the statement is false, write FALSE as well as the word or words that will make the statement true if they replaced the highlighted word or words in the original statement. If the statement is incomplete, write the word or words that will complete it.

1. Broca's area is in the inferior _____ cortex of the left hemisphere.

2. True or False: **Aphasia** is almost always associated with damage to the left hemisphere.

    A: _____

3. Although the symptoms of apraxia are bilateral, they are usually produced by unilateral _____ - hemisphere lesions.

4. Sinestrals are _____-handers.

5. The _____ test is an invasive test of speech lateralization that is often given to patients prior to neurosurgery.

6. The _____ test is a noninvasive test of language lateralization that was developed by Kimura.

7. True or False: Right-handed subjects tend to make larger speech movements with the **right side** of their mouths.

    A: _____

8. True or False: People tend to gesture during speech with the hand **ipsilateral** to their dominant language hemisphere.

    A: _____

9. In order to compare the reading ability of a split-brain patient's left and right hemispheres, it is necessary to use a device such as the _____ lens, which was developed by Zaidel.

10. In lab animals that have had a commissurotomy, visual information can be presented to the left hemisphere without the right hemisphere being aware of following surgical transection of the _____.

11. True or False: Left-handed subjects tend to have language skills localized to their **right hemisphere.**

    A: _____

12. Although the two hemispheres of a split-brain patient cannot directly communicate, they can sometimes influence one another indirectly by a method called _____.

Imagine that you are examining a split-brain patient. An image of a pencil is flashed in the left visual field of the person, and an image of an apple is simultaneously flashed in the right visual field . Answer "true" or "false" to each of the following statements.

13. The subject said that they had seen an apple. _____

14. When requested to feel several out-of-sight objects with their left hand and to select the object that they had seen, they picked a pencil. _____

15. When identifying the object that they had seen by simultaneously feeling two groups of out-of-sight objects, one group with each hand, they picked two pencils. _____

16. True or False: According to Levy and Sperry, the **left hemisphere** thinks in a synthetic mode.

    A: _____

17. True or False: According to Kimura, the **left hemisphere** is specialized for the control of fine motor movements, of which speech is but one particularly important example.

    A: _____

18. "Lateralization" refers to the relative control of a behavior by the left and right hemispheres; "_____" refers to the location within the hemispheres of the neural circuits responsible for the behavior.

Write "Broca's", "Wernicke's", or "conduction" in each of the following blanks.

19. a veritable word salad: _____ aphasia

20. damage just posterior to the left primary auditory area: _____ aphasia

21. damage to the arcuate fasciculus of the left hemisphere: _____ aphasia

22. damage to the left prefrontal lobe just anterior to the left primary motor face area of the motor homunculus: _____ aphasia

23. primarily receptive: _____ aphasia

24. primarily expressive: _____ aphasia

25. True or False: It has been suggested that the brains of females are lateralized **more** than the brains of males.

    A: _____

26. The Wernicke-Geschwind model is not a parallel model; it is a _____ model.

27. The CAT-scan results of neuropsychological patients with language-related problems have been analyzed in recent studies. The results of these studies have made two general points: that large anterior lesions of the left hemisphere are more likely to produce deficits in language _____ than are large posterior lesions, and that large posterior lesions of the left hemisphere are more likely to produce deficits in language _____ than are large anterior lesions.

28. There are two different procedures for reading aloud: a _____ procedure, which is based on memories of the pronunciations of specific words, and a _____ procedure, which is based on memories of general rules of pronunciation.

29. True or False: For the majority of people, there is a slight tendency for words presented to the right ear to be recognized **more readily** than those presented to in the left ear.

    A: _____

30. In surface dyslexia, the _____ procedure remains intact while the _____ procedure is disturbed; thus patients with surface dyslexia have difficulty in pronouncing irregular words like "yacht" and "sew" but have no difficulty in pronouncing regular nonwords such as "spleemer" and "twipple."

31. Petersen and his colleagues were able to conduct several tests in each subject because they injected radioactive _____ rather than radioactive gas.

32. Petersen and his colleagues were able to compare simultaneous patterns of blood flow in the two hemispheres because their injections were made _____ rather than into a carotid artery.

33. Although both Sperry's theory of the dual brain (that the hemispheres are each capable of independent cognitive activity) and the Wernicke-Geschwind model of language have both proven to be _____, only one has proven to be _____.

34. The ability of each hemisphere to simultaneously and independently engage in visual completion has been demonstrated using the _____ test.

35. True or False: McGlone found that **male victims** of unilateral strokes had deficits on both the verbal subtests and the performance subtests of the WAIS, regardless of which side the stroke was on.

          A: _____

C. Short Answer Section. In no more than 4 sentences, answer each of the following questions.

1. Discuss the saying "The right hand doesn't know what the left hand is doing" within the context of Sperry's split-brain studies.

2. Describe Petersen's dual-route theory of language.

3. What is confusing about the terms "Broca's aphasia" and "Wernicke's aphasia"?

4. Name each of the seven components of the Wernicke-Geschwind model and briefly describe the hypothetical function of each component.

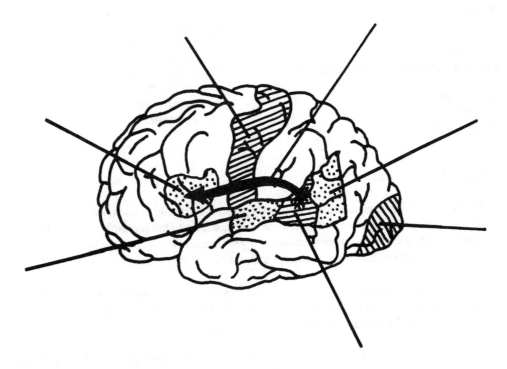

Mark your answers to the practice examination; the correct answers follow.   On the basis of your performance, plan the final stages of your studying.

Answers to Practice Examination

A. Multiple Choice Section

1. a
2. a
3. c
4. a, b
5. d
6. a, b, c
7. d
8. a

9. a, b, c, d
10. c
11. d
12. a, b, c, d
13. c
14. b
15. a

B. Modified True/False and Fill-in-the-Blank Section

1. frontal
2. true
3. left
4. left
5. sodium amytal
6. dichotic listening
7. true
8. F; contralateral
9. Z-lens
10. optic chiasm
11. F; left hemisphere
12. cross-cueing
13. True
14. True
15. False
16. F; analytic
17. true
18. localization

19. Wernicke's
20. Wernicke's
21. conduction
22. Broca's
23. Wernicke's
24. Broca's
25. F; less
26. serial
27. expression; comprehension
28. lexical; nonlexical
29. true
30. nonlexical; lexical
31. water
32. intravenously
33. important; correct (or equivalent)
34. chimeric-figures
35. F; females

C. Short Answer Section

1. Mention that when images are independently presented visually to each hemisphere, a person will use the left hemisphere will verbalize images shown to left hemisphere while they can use their left hand to pick out images shown to right hemisphere; the helping hand and cross cueing phenomena; the chimeric figures test; the use of the Z-lens.

2. Mention that practiced verbal responses move from sensory to motor cortex through Wernicke's area; novel responses move through frontal and cingulate cortex; key is that there are two routes for language comprehension/production.

3. Mention that these syndromes are rarely if ever seen in clear isolation; that damage restricted to Broca's area or Wernicke's area does not appear to have a lasting effect on language.

4. See Figure 16.10 from BIOPSYCHOLOGY

Chapter 17

THE BIOPSYCHOLOGY OF EMOTION, STRESS, AND MENTAL ILLNESS

I.   Jeopardy Study Items

With reference to Chapter 17 of BIOPSYCHOLOGY, write the correct answer to each of the following questions and the correct question for each of the following answers.

1.   A: *The Expression of Emotion in Man and Animals*

2. What is Darwin's theory of the evolution of emotional
    expression?

3.   A: the principle of antithesis

4.   What is the James-Lange theory?

5.   A: it viewed emotional experience and emotional expression
                                                             as parallel processes that are not causally related

6.   What is sham rage, and what did it suggest about the
hypothalamus?

7. What structures compose the limbic system?

8.   A: by removing their anterior temporal lobes

9. What are the symptoms of Kluver-Bucy syndrome?

10. What is the key difference between the James-Lange and
    Cannon-Bard theories in terms of the role of the ANS
    in emotion?

11.   A: polygraphy

12. Why is it difficult to evaluate the effectiveness of
    polygraphy.

13. What is the difference between the control-question
    technique and the guilty-knowledge technique?

14. Describe the evidence that facial expressions are a
    universal language for the conveyance of emotions.

15.   A: anger, surprise, sadness, disgust, fear, happiness

16. What is the facial feedback hypothesis?

17.   A: microexpressions

18. What is a Duchenne smile?

19.   A: zygomaticus major and obicularis oculi

20. How does the facial EMG provide a sensitive measure of
    emotion?

21. What evidence suggests that the common view that the
    right hemisphere is the emotional hemisphere is naive?

22.   A: prosody

23.   A: fear

24. What is ethoexperimental research?

25.   A: alpha males

26. What are the 3 general categories that have been used to
    describe the aggressive and defensive behaviors of rats?

27.   A: target-site concept

28. Why is the term "septal rage" misleading?

29. Describe the data supporting the hypothesis that
     aggressive behavior is attributable to the effects of
     testosterone.

30.   A: medial geniculate and amygdala

31. What is the role of the amygdala in fear conditioning?

32.   A: extinction

33.   A: amygdalectomy

34. What factors determine the magnitude of a stress
     response?

35. Describe the dual nature of the stress response.

36.   A: glucocorticoids

37. Which two physiological systems play key roles in the
     stress response?

38. What is a psychosomatic illness?

39. How does stress exacerbate the formation of gastric
    ulcers?

40.   A: Psychoneuroimmunology

41. Describe the two types of immune reactions that might be
    elicited by a foreign microorganism in the body.

42.   A: B cells

43. How does stress disrupt immune function?

44. What is the difference between a *psychoses* and a *neuroses?*

45.   A: schizophrenia

46. What are the symptoms of schizophrenia?

47. What evidence suggests that genetic factors influence
    schizophrenia?

48. What evidence suggests that stress plays a role in the activation of schizophrenic symptoms?

49.   A: chlorpromazine

50.   A: reserpine

51. What is the dopamine theory of schizophrenia?

52. How does chlorpromazine influence dopamine transmission?

53.   A: haloperidol

54. What is the key difference between phenothiazine and butyrophenone antipsychotic drugs>

55. What are the effects of clozapine?

56. What parts of the brain are involved in schizophrenia?

57. Describe the difference between *positive* and *negative* symptoms of schizophrenia.

58. What are the two types of affective illness?

59. What is the difference between reactive and endogenous depression?

60. Describe the evidence for the hypothesis that genetics plays a key role in the development of affective disorders.

61.   A: iproniazid

62. What is the cheese effect?

63. What are the effects of imipramine?

64.   A: lithium

65. Why was the medical community so slow to accept Cade's claim that lithium was an effective treatment for mania?

66. How does Prozac exert its psychoactive effects?

67. What is the monoamine hypothesis of depression?

68. What are the weaknesses of the monoamine theory of depression?

69. What is the dexamethaxone suppression test?

70. What are the symptoms of anxiety?

71. What are the four major classes of anxiety disorders?

72.   A: Librium and Valium

73. What is the mechanism of action for the benzodiazepines?

74.   A: buspirone

75. What brain structure is believed to play a key role in anxiety disorders?

Once you have completed the jeopardy study items, study them. Practice bidirectional studying; make sure that you know the correct answer to every question and the correct question for every answer.

II.   Essay Study Questions

Using Chapter 17 of BIOPSYCHOLOGY, write an outline of the answer to each of the following essay study questions.

1. Discuss the idea that emotional expression is related to emotional experience.

2. Describe how Darwin's theory of the evolution of emotion accounts for the evolution of threat displays in animals.

3. According to the pop-science industry, emotion resides in the right hemisphere. Discuss.

4. Compare fear, anxiety, and stress. Describe the role of the adrenal cortex and the adrenal medulla in the stress response.

5. What is psychoneuroimmunology? Discuss psychoneuroimmunologic research on stress.

6. What is an ethoexperimental approach to research? Describe two examples.

7. What evidence suggests that the physiological basis of social aggression is distinct from the physiological bases of defensive attack and predatory aggression?

8. Describe the monoamine hypothesis of affective illness. What are the shortcomings of this idea?.

9. Describe the major steps in the development of the current dopamine theory of schizophrenia.

When you have answered the essay study questions, memorize your outlines to prepare for your upcoming examination.

III.   Practice Examination

After completing most of your studying of Chapter 17, but at least 24 hours before your formal examination, write the following practice examination.

A. Multiple-Choice Section. Circle the correct answer for each question; *REMEMBER that some questions may have more than one correct answer.*

1. The emotional response to threat is called:

    a. stress.
    b. anxiety.
    c. fear.
    d. general adaptation.

2. The feeling of fear in the absence of any direct threat is called:

    a. fear.
    b. mania.
    c. stress.
    d. anxiety.

3. Glucocorticoids are released by the:

    a. adrenal cortex.
    b. adrenal gland.
    c. neocortex.
    d. anterior pituitary.

4. Pharmacological evidence supports the idea that anxiety is due to deficits in:

    a. corticosteroid activity.
    b. GABAergic activity.
    c. pituitary activity.
    d. serotonergic activity.

5. According to Albert and his colleagues, the failure to find a consistent correlation between human aggression and testosterone levels is due to the fact that:

    a. human aggression is heavily socialized.
    b. researchers often fail to distinguish between defensive aggression and social aggression.
    c. human aggression does not decline in castrated males.
    d. aggression increases testosterone levels, and not the other way around.

6. The limbic system includes the:

    a. hippocampus, amygdala and septum
    b. pituitary, adrenal gland, and thalamus.
    c. hypothalamus, olfactory bulb, and mammillary body
    d. gonads, optic chiasm, and cerebellum.

7. According to Eckman and his colleagues, the relationship between emotions and facial expression:

    a. is similar across cultures.
    b. is based on just six primary emotions.
    c. can easily be falsified so that even an expert cannot discern a person's true feelings.
    d. exists only when a person first feels the emotion; the emotion cannot be elicited simply by adopting the appropriate facial expression.

8. The symptoms of schizophrenia include:

    a. low self-esteem, despair, and suicide.
    b. delusions, hallucinations, odd behavior, incoherent thought, and inappropriate affect.
    c. fear that persists in the absence of any direct threat.
    d. tachycardia, hypertension, and high corticosteroid levels.

9. Auditory fear conditioning depends upon direct or indirect neural pathways from the:

    a. medial geniculate nucleus of the thalamus to primary auditory cortex.
    b. from the ear to the medial geniculate nucleus of the thalamus.
    c. from the medial geniculate nucleus of the thalamus to the amygdala.
    d. from the amygdala to the primary auditory cortex.

10. The monoamine hypothesis of affective illness is:

    a. based on the idea that depressed patients have increased monoaminergic activity and manic patients have decreased monoaminergic activity.
    b. compromised by the fact that antidepressants immediately increase central monoamine levels, but the therapeutic effect does not appear for several weeks.
    c. based on the observation that lithium is not an effective antidepressant.
    d. based upon strong correlations between measures on monoaminergic activity and affective state in patients who suffer from depression.

11. Selye's conceptualization of the stress response:

    a. marked a key link between psychological and physiological well-being.
    b. focused on activation of the sympathetic nervous system.
    c. focused on activation of the anterior pituitary adrenal cortex system.
    d. emphasized the effects of both acute and chronic stress on an organism.

12. Stress-induced alterations in the function of the immune system are:

    a. clinically significant, although demonstrating this link has been difficult.
    b. related to corticosterone or norepinephrine-induced alterations in T-cell and B-cell activity.
    c. difficult to demonstrate, even in the laboratory.
    d. due to inoculation of stressed individuals.

13. Benzodiazepines like Valium and Librium are:

    a. widely prescribed antipsychotic drugs.
    b. believed to alter neural function by their agonistic action at GABA-A receptors.
    c. prescribed for their hypnotic, anticonvulsant, and muscle relaxant properties.
    d. the only know antianxiety drugs.

B. Modified True-False and Fill-in-the Blank Section. If the statement is true, write TRUE in the blank provided. If the statement is false, write FALSE as well as the word or words that will make the statement true if they replaced the highlighted word or words in the original statement. If the statement is incomplete, write the word or words that will complete it.

1. According to Darwin, expressions of emotion evolve from behaviors that indicate what an animal is
   _____.

2. According to Darwin's principle of _____, opposite messages are often signaled by opposite movements and postures.

   Next to each of the following descriptions, write J-L (James-Lange) or C-B (Cannon-Bard).

3. _____   The first major physiological theory of emotion; proposed in 1884.

4. _____   The experience of emotion results from the brain's perception of the body's reaction to emotional stimuli.

5. _____   Emotional expression and emotional experience are parallel processes that have not direct causal relation.

6. True or False: The study of sham rage in decerebrate animals implicated the **hypothalmus** in aggressive behavior.
   A: _____

7. The amygdala, hippocampus, septum, fornix, olfactory bulb, mammillary body, and cingulate cortex are considered to be part of the _____.

8. Bilateral destruction of the anterior portions of the temporal lobes often results in a condition called _____ syndrome.

9. True or False: Enlarged adrenal glands, gastric ulcers, and suppressed immune function are generally caused by exposure to **acute stress.**

   A: _____

10. _____ is a method of interrogation in which autonomic nervous system indices of emotion are used to infer the truthfulness of a subject's responses.

11. The most effective polygraphic technique is the _____ technique.

12. According to Eckman and Friesen (1975), the facial expressions of anger, fear, happiness, surprise, sadness, and disgust are called _____.

13. Movement of _____ muscle distinguishes fake smiles from genuine smiles.

14. Although it is often portrayed as such, it is a mistake to think of emotion as a single global faculty that resides in the _____ hemisphere.

15. Gastric ulcers are believed to be caused by an increase in the secretion of _____ and a decrease in the efficiency of the _____.

16. Lymphocytes that respond specifically to combat particular kinds of invading microorganisms are called _____.

17. B cells manufacture _____.

18. B cells and T cells are _____.

Next to each of the following write "alpha male" or "male intruder."

19.   Piloerection: _____

20.   Lateral attack: _____

21.   Boxing: _____

22.   Back biting: _____

Next to each of the following drugs write the psychological disorder that it is effective against.

23.   Lithium: _____

24.   Chlorpromazine: _____

25.   Iproniazid: _____

26.   Benzodiazepines: _____

27.   Haloperidol: _____

28.   Reserpine: _____

29.   Buspirone: _____

30.   Clozapine: _____

31.   Imipramine: _____

32. True or False: The elevated plus maze is used to assess the **antidepressant** effects of drugs.

A: _____

33. Chlorpromazine is a _____ transmitter at dopamine synapses.

34. Both phenothiazines and butyrophenones induce _____ side effects.

35. The effectiveness of clozapine has implicated _____ receptors in schizophrenia.

36. The first tricyclic antidepressant was _____.

37. True or False: Excessive secretion of **gastric mucus** is associated with the development of gastric ulcers.

A: _____

C. Short Answer Section. In no more than 4 sentences, answer each of the following questions.

1. Summarize the results of research on the relationship between facial expression and emotions.

2. What is an amygdalectomy? Why is its utility in the treatment of aggressive disorders questionable?

3. Comment on the statement "Human aggression is not related to testosterone levels.".

4. Describe the drugs that are used in the treatment of schizophrenia. What do they suggest about the neural basis of this disease?

5. Discuss evidence that supports the hypothesis that anxiety is mediated by GABAergic mechanisms

Mark your answers to the practice examination; the correct answers follow. On the basis of your performance, plan the final stages of your studying.

Answers to Practice Examination

A. Multiple Choice Section

1. c
2. d
3. a
4. b, d
5. b
6. a, c
7. a, b

8. b
9. b, c
10. b
11. a, c, d
12. a, b, c
13. b, c

B. Modified True/False and Fill-in-the-Blank Section

1. likely to do next.
2. antithesis
3. J-L
4. J-L
5. C-B
6. F; decorticate
7. limbic system
8. Kluver-Bucy
9. F; chronic stress
10. polygraphy
11. guilty-knowledge
12. primary emotions
13. obicularis oculi
14. right
15. stomach secretions; mucus barrier
16. T-cells
17. antibodies
18. lymphocytes
19. alpha male

20. alpha male
21. male intruder
22. alpha male
23. bipolar affective disorder
24. schizophrenia
25. unipolar affective disorder (or depression)
26. anxiety disorder
27. schizophrenia
28. schizophrenia
29. anxiety disorder
30. schizophrenia
31. unipolar affective disorder (or depression)
32. F; anxiolytic (or antianxiety)
33. false
34. parkinsonian
35. D_3
36. imipramine
37. hydrochloric acid

C. Short Answer Section

1. Mention evidence for the universality of facial expression and emotion; for the six primary facial expressions; for the facial feedback hypothesis; and the role than voluntary control exerts over facial expression

2. Mention the bilateral surgical removal of the amygdala; the fact that this surgery is not universally effective; the fact that it produces a general blunting of affect rather than a specific reduction in aggressive behaviors.

3. Mention link between social aggression and testosterone in nonhuman species; that human evidence is weaker, but may reflect a focus on defensive aggression

4. Mention that these drugs block dopamine receptors, suggesting that excessive dopaminergic activity underlies schizophrenia.

5. Mention fact that many antianxiety drugs alter GABA-A activity; however, note that effectiveness of buspirone suggests alterations in serotonergic activity as well.

6. See Figure 17.9 in BIOPSYCHOLOGY.